WARFARE
IN FEUDAL EUROPE
730-1200

WARFARE
IN FEUDAL EUROPE
730-1200

JOHN BEELER

Professor of History
The University of North Carolina
at Greensboro

Cornell University Press | ITHACA & LONDON

U
37
.B44

First published 1971 by Cornell University Press.
Published in the United Kingdom by Cornell University Press Ltd.,
2–4 Brook Street, London W1Y 1AA.

International Standard Book Number 0-8014-0638-2
Library of Congress Catalog Card Number 74-148018

PRINTED IN THE UNITED STATES OF AMERICA
BY VAIL-BALLOU PRESS, INC.

To the memory of

CARL STEPHENSON

Preface

The revival of interest in military history has done much to rescue medieval military institutions and practices from undeserved oblivion. Particularly during the last ten years, books and monographs dealing with all aspects of medieval warfare have been appearing at a gratifying rate. Most of these new studies are highly specialized, and the only survey of a general nature in English is Sir Charles Oman's two-volume work, *A History of the Art of War in the Middle Ages* (London, 1924), which is still valuable but now over forty-five years old. It is partly to fill this gap that I have been encouraged to write the present volume.

To Professors Robin Higham of Kansas State University and C. W. Hollister of the University of California at Santa Barbara I am indebted for numerous helpful suggestions. I thank the library staff of the University of North Carolina at Greensboro, especially Mrs. Elizabeth J. Holder, Miss Mary Robert Seawall, and Miss Emilie Mills, for invaluable aid cheerfully given. To Anne, my wife, and to my daughter Hazel I am in debt for, among other things, help in typing a draft from my longhand manuscript, and to Mrs. Louise Mills for typing the final draft.

John Beeler

Greensboro, North Carolina
St. Oswald's Day, 1970

Contents

Maps

Introduction

Possibly because of the obscurity that shrouds much of the period in European history usually labeled "feudal," few attempts have been made to describe or explain its warfare. Much is known about feudalism as a social, political, and military institution; we know something about how the feudal system produced fighting men, but little research has been undertaken to find out how these warriors were employed on campaign or in battle.

The primary reason for this gap in our knowledge of the history of warfare is the generally unsatisfactory nature of the surviving sources. A few capitularies deal with the military organization of the Carolingian empire; occasional charters in France, England, Italy, and elsewhere mention, incidentally, conditions of military service. The Domesday Book and royal charters have something to say about such subjects as castles and municipal defenses. The archaeologist can tell us much about the early fortifications of the feudal age. But this kind of evidence is not of much help in determining the sources of the troops, in reconstructing campaigns or battles, or in ascertaining the strategy or tactics used by a particular general on a spe-

cific occasion. And, unfortunately, the narrative accounts
are frequently useless. For example, the two modern historians who have written in detail about the rather obscure
battle of Cassel in Flanders (22 February 1071) totally
disagree over which of the contending parties held the
castle of Cassel at the start of the battle. Each scholar
used exactly the same sources, which are so ambiguous
that two competent historians drew from them quite different conclusions.

In feudal Europe there were no military writers per se,
and little specifically military writing. Narrative history
was written by the only literate class of the day—the
clergy, principally the monks. Understandably, they had
little comprehension of military matters and even less
interest in the complexities of strategy and tactics. Western Europe had to wait until the Renaissance for military
writers of the caliber of the emperors Maurice, Nicephorus
II Phocas, and Leo VI (the Wise), whose works give us
a broad view of Byzantine military institutions and practices. Another difficulty is the extraordinary diversity of
feudal military practices, which were as varied as those
of modern times. Feudal warfare was in the process of
evolution and modification for nearly five centuries, and
its vestiges survived much longer.

While military feudalism was fully developed in the Ile
de France, elsewhere it was modified by a great variety of
factors. Thus in places where it was indigenous feudal
warfare was not the same as it was in areas where it was
consciously adopted or was imposed by foreign settlers or
invaders. There were also an almost infinite number of
local variations. In northern France, for example, feudalism was theoretically everywhere essentially the same.

But actually the military capabilities of, let us say, the king of France differed markedly from those of the count of Flanders; a tremendous advantage lay with the count.

My plan for dealing with this complexity is to discuss military feudalism as it originated and developed in the Frankish kingdom of the Carolingians, and as it operated during the early Capetian period in the Ile de France and the feudal principalities of northern France. Next I follow feudal developments, in roughly chronological order, in those states where feudalism was consciously imported— lower Italy and Sicily, England, and Crusader Syria. Then I treat those lands in which the military structure revealed some feudal characteristics, but where, for a variety of reasons, military institutions were never more than super- ficially feudalized—southern France, Christian Spain, cen- tral and northern Italy, and Germany. I attempt to show how such factors as native military institutions, the pattern of landholding, economic structure, manpower problems, and the like worked to modify feudal military institutions and practices.

It is likely that scholars have been turned away from the study of feudal warfare by a general misconception of its nature. Indeed, the term "feudal warfare" has been so misused by historians over the last century that its proper meaning has been almost lost or forgotten. The adjective "feudal" ought to be applied only to the wars and cam- paigns fought during the age of feudalism. But so uni- versal is the belief that military operations in the feudal period were confused, aimless, and incompetently led that historians often use the word to describe actions meriting these strictures regardless of the period in which they took place. This does a grave injustice to the fighting men of the early Middle Ages. By no means were all military operations between the eighth and twelfth centuries confused and lacking in rational objectives. Moreover, the proportion of competent generals was probably as high in the feudal age as it has ever been.

Many misconceptions have arisen from a lack of understanding of the true nature of feudal warfare. While this lack stems in large part from the scarcity of contemporary accounts about how armies were formed and employed, it is also due to a failure to make full use of the available information. Much has been written about the social, political, and economic aspects of feudalism. Scholars are generally agreed that feudal society had its roots in the military necessities of the eighth and ninth centuries, when the old infantry levy of the Germanic peoples proved no longer capable of meeting the demands placed upon it, and that a new form of military efficiency based on mounted service slowly evolved. But little has been done to find out how the "feudal" troops were used in war. Only recently have scholars begun to show an interest in the military aspects of feudal society; the works of C. W. Hollister, Michael Müller-Wille, Michael Powicke, and J. F. Verbruggen are indicative of the new trend in medieval military scholarship. The constitutional and legal aspects of feudal service have been more than adequately considered by such eminent scholars as J. H. Round, Sir Frank Stenton, Marc Bloch, and F. L. Ganshof, and the interested reader can refer to their works with confidence. No attempt is made in the present study to provide such information unless it will enable the student to understand the feudal chain of command. Nor do I give a blow-by-blow account of all the wars fought between the eighth and twelfth centuries.

One purpose of a book of this kind should be to stimulate the reader to further exploration on his own. For this reason a single description of a particular type of action has been deemed sufficient for a given area. For example, Richard the Lion-Hearted, large as he bulks in the romances, had very little influence on the military practices of western Europe. His celebrated victory over Saladin at Arsuf (1191) was but another example of the type of running engagement characteristic of warfare in the Latin east. Since I describe in detail the much more interesting Busra campaign of 1147, it seems unnecessary to say anything about Arsuf.

This book is concerned primarily with such subjects as the bases on which feudal service was exacted, the mustering and composition of armies and their subsequent operations in the field, and the quality and qualifications of their commanders. It would be useful to know something about the logistical problems faced by feudal generals, but apart from occasional references little information is available on how armies were supplied and equipped until well into the thirteenth century. All soldiers were required to furnish their own arms and equipment, so it is bootless to inquire into the industry—which must generally have been local—that provided the armor and weapons with which feudal armies took the field before the stage when governments were prepared to equip their troops. Attention is given to the construction of fortifications and the devices used to garrison them.

Any attempt to put a time limit on a particular historical period is arbitrary and bound to draw criticism. I have chosen the beginning of the thirteenth century because by this time commanders were raising their most reliable units by means that were certainly not "feudal." All too many students—and teachers—tend to equate "feudal" with "medieval," although the terms are by no means synonymous. Edward I, the Black Prince, Emperor Frederick II, Charles of Anjou, Henry V, and John Zisca simply do not belong in a book about feudal warfare. So *before* beginning to discuss feudal warfare, I had best define just what I mean by the term "feudal." A feudal soldier (perhaps warrior or fighter would be a more accurate designation) was an individual who in return for a grant—usually of land—known first as a benefice, later as a fief, contracted to serve in the armed forces of his lord at his own expense for a period of time. At first the benefice was not hereditary and the period of service was probably unlimited, but eventually the fief became heritable and a fairly standard service of forty days per year in time of war became customary. A feudal army, then, would be an army in which all or most of the troops were serving at their own expense in return for fiefs, and feudal warfare would usually, but not always, involve opposing forces composed of troops raised in such a manner. All troops raised in other ways, or paid in some other fashion, must be described as nonfeudal. The term "antifeudal," which some authorities use, is essentially meaningless, since no one from the eighth to the thirteenth century would have been aware that the use of paid troops was in any way detrimental to the established order. The extent to which the term "feudal" can be applied to the armed conflict of these centuries is one of the problems examined in the following pages.

WARFARE
IN FEUDAL EUROPE
730-1200

1

Warfare in
Carolingian Europe

The origins of those political, social, and military institutions known collectively as feudal can be traced far
back into the history of the later Roman Empire and of
primitive German society. They have been subjected to
intense scrutiny by scholars, whose interpretations of the
scanty evidence have given rise to heated, sometimes
bitter controversy. It is not my purpose to trace in detail
the development of feudal institutions but to show how
and why the elements of personal dependence and dependent land tenure which were characteristic of late
Roman and early Germanic societies eventually merged
and were utilized by the Carolingians and their successors
to put adequate numbers of soldiers into the field.

The sources of the element of personal dependence, in
what came to be known as the lord-vassal relationship,
can be traced back to both late Roman and early Germanic times. In almost every society there is a double
tendency at work as the weak seek the protection and support of the strong, and the strong seek to extend their
domination over the weak. The late imperial period,

roughly the third to the fifth century, saw the rapid extension of an institution known as patronage (patrocinium),
in which powerful and influential men (*patrones*) surrounded themselves with groups of followers and hangers-
on known as clients. The insecurity of the times led many
free laborers and small landowners voluntarily to seek the
aid of those who could offer support and protection. In
return they agreed to supply such services as the patron
might need or demand. The service might be agricultural,
it might be personal, or it might be military service in the
private armies maintained by many of the powerful
nobles. Similarly, in Gaul each Celtic chieftain had a body
of retainers for whom he provided food and shelter and on
whom he depended for essential administrative and military services. Indeed, the word "vassal" (*vassus*) is ulti-
mately Celtic in derivation. In early Germanic society, the
institution which emphasized personal dependence was
the war band, the comitatus. The dependence of the individual warrior on the war chief was sealed by a ceremonial
oath of allegiance, a feature of great significance in later
feudalism. It is not surprising that when the Germanic
peoples settled in large numbers in the western provinces
of the empire, similar institutions had a tendency to co-
alesce and the fusion of the Roman patrocinium and the
German comitatus strengthened two elements that later
became characteristic of the feudal system: the formal
dependence of the weaker on the stronger man, and the
performance of some service—often military—in return
for personal security.

Another characteristic of fully developed feudalism was
dependent land tenure: a man held and used land from
which he derived the profit (or usufruct), although legal

title belonged to another man. The chief antecedent was the Roman practice known as precarium. It is difficult to describe the precarium without getting involved in all sorts of legal complexities. Strictly speaking, a man would make a petition, or prayer (precarium), to a landowner for a plot of land to cultivate. The prayer, if granted, was, at least in theory, free of all cost to the petitioner. The owner only lent the land for use, and since he retained full title to it, he could reclaim it at any time, but this was merely a legal fiction. In practice, the precarium was a lease of land for rent, under a contract, written or otherwise agreed upon between the grantor and the lessee. Although the owner could legally evict the tenant at any time, there was customarily no trouble if the rent was paid regularly or other obligations were met as specified in the contract. It was even possible to pass such a tenement down to one's heirs despite its technically precarious nature.

Again, because of the insecurity of the fourth and fifth centuries, not only the free laborer seeking security sought land on precarious tenure. Small landowners, pressed by debt and crushing taxation or spurred by fear of agressive neighbors, frequently surrendered title to their lands to some powerful landowner and received it back as a precarium. Although the original owner lost legal title to his lands, his tenure was reasonably secure. The new owner increased his domain, the former owner was assured of protection, and the arrangement benefited both parties to the agreement.

The church also became involved in precarial relationships during these troubled centuries. Many individuals were willing to transfer title to their lands to the church in return for assurance of salvation. Often such donors retained the use of their lands on precarial tenure during their lifetimes. As its lands grew in extent, the church found it profitable to grant much of its holdings to individuals as precaria, since the canon law forbade any permanent alienation of church property. Thus both lay and ecclesiastical owners had an interest in extending the use of the precarium.

During this period of confusion there was no connection, legal or otherwise, between the personal dependence of the patronage system (patrocinium) and the system of dependent land tenure (precarium). But in an age when money payments were gradually being replaced by payments in kind, a landowner without extensive money resources might readily reward a faithful servitor with a grant of land. This process could work two ways. Whether a client was rewarded with a grant of land on precarious tenure or whether the holder of a precarium became also a personal dependent—a client—the trend toward feudal relationships was accelerated. The Germanic invasions of the fifth and sixth centuries only intensified a development which had begun two hundred years earlier. The civil wars during the Merovingian period of the sixth and seventh centuries increased the need of almost every segment of society for protection. Kings and great landed magnates surrounded themselves with bands (*trustes*) of faithful followers (*fideles, antrustiones*), and the Roman patrocinium and the German comitatus merged in a practice known as commendation (*commendatio*). The man who commended himself to a lord was now required to perform a ceremonial act of homage, a practice of German origin which involved a promise of loyalty. Eventually the church intervened to require an additional oath of fealty, sworn on the Scriptures or saints' relics. "Fealty," derived from the Latin *fidelitas,* meant specifically the fidelity of a vassal to his lord.

In the meantime the use of the precarium had spread throughout the west, although it was by no means accepted universally. The church in particular found it a useful device for bringing its extensive lands under cultivation. At some time during the Merovingian period the form of the word changed, and the feminine *precaria* was commonly used. Grants of *precariae* were now more specific, being made for fixed periods of time or for the lifetime of the recipient or of his children. Quite early in the process attempts on the part of tenants to make these grants hereditary can be detected. During the course of the eighth century the term *precaria* was itself replaced by another Latin word, *beneficium* (benefice). Essentially there was no difference between the *precaria* and the benefice. They were leases of land for specific periods of time in return for rent or services. Such leases were revocable if the lord felt that the terms of the grant had not been carried out. Custom, to some extent, restricted the arbitrary expulsion of an occupant, and, of course, a lord had to be in a position to use force in order to dispossess a recalcitrant tenant.

It must be emphasized that at this stage of development, there was no necessary connection between vassalage and the possession of a benefice. A vassal might hold a benefice, but if he did not, he was maintained at the court of his lord or, more likely, he had land of his own (known as an allod). Conversely, the holder of a benefice was not necessarily a vassal. But it seems certain that in the late

Merovingian and early Carolingian periods there was a closer connection between vassalage and benefice than had existed between patronage and precarium in late imperial times. As the economy of western Europe became more purely agricultural and money disappeared from circulation, it became increasingly difficult to pay officials or reward vassals. In these circumstances, the grant of a benefice was the logical means by which payment could be made. It is also obvious that only kings, great nobles, and the church—men or institutions well endowed with land—could afford to adopt such a policy. Thus, when a vassal received a benefice, the elements of personal dependence and dependent land tenure became definitely associated. And when the Merovingian kings began to appoint their own vassals to official positions—as dukes and counts—and paid them with benefices, public office also became associated with landholding and vassalage. Finally, about 730, during the administration of the Frankish state by Charles Martel, military service began to be required of benefice holders.

It is now necessary to trace the developments which made this requirement possible and even essential. Not much is known about the early military institutions and practices of the Germans. All free men, apparently, were subject to military service. The comitatus consisted of elite warriors assembled around a chosen war chief. As is often the case with primitive peoples, early German tactics consisted of a series of wild rushes which were relied upon to carry the day. If these failed, the attackers became demoralized and faded away into the forest. The leader of the war band was supposed to set an example of courage in battle; the members of the comitatus were not supposed to leave the battlefield while the chief was still present nor to survive him if he fell, but none of these conditions seems to have been universally observed. In general the Germans fought as infantry. Only the Goths, who dwelt for several generations on the steppes of southern Russia, learned the art of fighting on horseback.

During the first three centuries of the Christian era, when the imperial frontier was stabilized along the Rhine and the Danube, the Germans were in constant contact with the Romans. In the third century, for a variety of reasons which cannot be detailed here, large numbers of Germans began to enter Roman military service in several ways. Many were enlisted as individual recruits in the legionary formations. Others entered the imperial service in organized bands, known as *foederati,* under their own commanders, who then became Roman officers. The large-scale enlistment of Germans tended to reduce the efficiency of the Roman army, while it had the effect of improving the military capabilities of the Germans. In the end, the Roman army became barbarized along with the western provinces of the empire. The legions—largely German—won their last great victory over the Germans near Strasbourg in 357.

By the middle of the fifth century several barbarian peoples had established states in the former western provinces of the empire. Most of these had too narrow a military base for permanence. Ostrogothic Italy, Visigothic Spain, and Vandalic Africa were governed by military aristocracies in command of what amounted to small Germanic armies of occupation. As the Germans became Romanized, they lost their zeal for fighting and were unable to oppose vigorously the Byzantines and Moslems who established themselves in Italy and Spain. During the so-called Dark Ages, what had survived of the old military traditions finally disappeared in the west. The Romans themselves had abandoned the infantry tradition under pressure of the mobile, lightly equipped Germans and the mounted Goths, and during the period of the late empire, the Romans had emphasized the cavalry arm.

For a short time during the early sixth century it seemed possible that there might be a revitalization of the infantry tradition. The Germans, including the Franks, were essentially a people of the forest, which precluded the extensive use of cavalry. When the Franks moved south and west into Gaul, they were light-armed infantry. They wore no body armor, but were protected by oval shields. Their arms consisted of javelins similar to the Roman pila, swords, and daggers. The Franks were also noted for their skill with the battle-axe (francisca), a heavy, well-balanced weapon. They had learned to throw the francisca while on the run, and the axes were hurled at the enemy just before contact was made. The evidence is so fragmentary and unsatisfactory that it is impossible to do more than guess at Frankish military organization at this stage. Probably, it had not evolved beyond the elementary massing of warriors in a dense phalanx. The inadequacy of this sort of formation was demonstrated in bloody fashion in the middle of the sixth century. When the Franks engaged a Byzantine army containing both infantry and cavalry at Casilinum (modern Capua) in Italy in 554, the results were disastrous. The unwieldy infantry phalanx was surrounded, and the Byzantine horse archers shot down the virtually defenseless Franks almost as if they were engaging in target practice. Even after this catastrophe, the

Franks were slow to abandon their traditional mode of fighting.

The character of Merovingian military institutions as Frankish society was stabilized, is clearer. Unlike the populations of other Germanic kingdoms, all free people resident in the Frankish state, whether Franks or not, were obligated to serve in the host which could be called out by the king at any time. As the economic structure became predominantly agrarian, military service tended to be closely associated with landholding. Each free household owed the service of a man with complete arms and equipment, and this military obligation soon became hereditary. The Frankish army thus became a levy of free men serving at the king's will, under the command of his local representative, the count.

The social and military origin of the feudal knight is not, however, in this mass levy of free men (*landwehr*), but in elite warrior groups, the *comitati*. These gradually evolved into select bands of fighting men maintained by kings and great magnates, and they became the nucleus of the Frankish aristocracy. Slowly the members of this class learned the lessons of such disasters as Casilinum and began to adopt the use of armor. By the beginning of the eighth century, the personal followings of kings and great nobles may have ridden to battle but dismounted to fight. The evidence on this point, however, is scanty and somewhat contradictory.

But two developments, completely unrelated, made the formation of truly effective cavalry both possible and necessary. The first was the introduction of the stirrup in the early eighth century. This was a technological advance of great significance, for it increased tremendously the efficiency of the mounted trooper. The rider, firmly seated, was able to deliver a powerful thrust with his lance, or he could rise in his stirrups to use his sword with greater leverage. Hitherto, cavalry tactics were restricted to archery or to hurling lances and javelins. The infantry of the Macedonian phalanx or the legions of Rome never had to face such firmly seated horsemen; the hastily mustered, largely untrained Frankish foot soldier was much less capable, and his weapons were ineffective against the armor of the horseman. It was difficult to topple him from the saddle, and not until the time of the Swiss halberdier in the fourteenth century could infantry again cope with cavalry on equal terms at close quarters. The second development was the appearance north of the Pyrenees of columns of mounted Moorish raiders. Attempts have been made to show that it was the adoption of the stirrup that triggered the marked shift in emphasis from infantry to cavalry formations, but the argument does not bear close scrutiny.[1]

The evolution of military techniques is usually a slow process unless there is some overriding consideration which compels an immediate change in concepts. It seems likely that the stirrup made its first appearance in western Europe in the early decades of the eighth century, but it by no means prompted all European peoples, to take to fighting on horseback. The Saxons and the English, for example, continued to rely on the customary infantry levies for centuries. The army which faced Duke William

[1] For a detailed discussion of this question, see Lynn White, Jr., "Stirrup, Mounted Shock Combat, Feudalism, and Chivalry," in *Medieval Technology and Social Change* (Oxford, 1962), pp. 1–38, and notes, pp. 135–153.

of Normandy at Hastings in 1066 consisted entirely of foot soldiers, and as late as 1214 the Saxon contingents in the imperial army at Bouvines contained a majority of infantrymen. The rapid—almost precipitate for a military change—conversion of the Frankish army from infantry to cavalry must, then, have been due to some military threat which could have been met in no other way. The only serious menace came from the expansionist Moorish state in Spain.

The most pressing problem for the Frankish rulers was how to respond to the obvious necessity for changing the nature and equipment of their armed forces. Acquiring a horse, lance, sword, shield, and armor was an expensive proposition, one that far exceeded the resources of the ordinary free man. The free peasant, faced with the day-to-day struggle for mere existence imposed upon him by the crude agricultural methods of the period, had little time to devote to mastering the sophisticated techniques of fighting on horseback. Effective use of this equipment required continual practice. Handling a shield and a lance or sword while at the same time managing a horse was a skill that could be achieved only through long experience and rigid training. To acquire such expertise soldiers had to be rich enough to afford horses and arms, and they also had to be free from the need to work for a living.

Furthermore, the economic decline which characterized the half-millenium from the fifth to the tenth century meant that there was virtually no surplus capital available to the ruler of a state. At this time no western European monarch had at his command an organized, literate civil service which could deal with fiscal matters on a state-wide basis. The king of the Franks was expected to main-

tain his family, his personal retinue, and the officers of
state from the revenues of the royal domain. It is not surprising that no surplus was available that could be devoted to the recruitment, training, and maintenance of a
professional mounted army. If Charles Martel was to have
at his disposal a significant number of troopers, he had to
find land for each one and the labor to cultivate it.

About 730, Charles began to exploit the benefice, which
had been used for centuries for other than military purposes. The new practice had been adopted so recently
that it had no effect on the action at Tours in 733, but
the inability of the Franks to gain any real advantage
from the victory over the Moslems doubtless gave impetus
to the trend toward mounted service. The Frankish leader
recruited able warriors who were required to swear absolute fidelity to him. They thus became his vassals—*vassi
dominici*. To each one he granted a benefice in the form of
an estate of sufficient size to support him and to enable
him to fulfill his military obligations. The benefice was
held as long as the grantee served Charles well in his military capacity. At the vassals' death, or if he became in-
capacitated or violated his oath, the grant was revoked,
and the benefice was regranted to someone who would
assume the military obligation that was attached to the
land. Soon it became apparent that the royal demesne was
inadequate to provide as many benefices as were necessary. Moreover, too extensive an alienation of the demesne—the granting away of crown lands—would diminish the already limited resources of the government.
Charles then began to look with greedy eyes at the vast
estates of the Gallic church. The church had long been accustomed to granting lands on beneficial tenure. Despite

their violent protests, bishops and abbots were compelled to grant benefices to warriors on condition that the soldiers serve Charles as mounted troops. In theory, at least, these benefices were held of the ecclesiastical institution from whose lands they were granted, and the land—again in theory—remained church land, but actually it passed under the control of Charles. He thus solved his military problems and greatly influenced the later development of feudalism. For one thing, he inextricably associated the concept of military service with landholding and vassalage. He also ensured that the church would be caught up in the toils of feudalism; the military bishops and abbots of the feudal age are a demonstrable consequence of Charles's policies. The short-range results were more tangible. It was the mobility given the Franks by the innovations of Charles Martel, rather than the tenacious defensive stand of the Frankish infantry at Tours, that won eventual victory over the Moors in a long struggle that did not end until 759. The mobile troops also enabled him to begin the conquest of the Saxons and to lessen the danger along his eastern frontier.

The transition to a primary reliance on mounted service was not accomplished all at once. The campaigns of Charles's son Pepin (741–768) were likely fought by troops who rode to battle but still dismounted to fight. The Moors were driven back across the Pyrenees; the Bavarians on the upper Danube were compelled to acknowledge Frankish overlordship, and two campaigns were conducted against the Lombards in Italy. All this suggests a degree of mobility not to be found in the old infantry levy, but the evidence indicates that as late as the reign of Charlemagne (768–814), a considerable portion of the army still consisted of foot soldiers. The proportion steadily decreased, however, and by the end of the reign, the Frankish host seems to have consisted largely of mounted contingents marching under the command of their lords. The many successful campaigns fought by Charlemagne on widely separated frontiers were made possible in large part by the increasing reliance on mounted troops, although the infantry levy continued to be employed.

From those curious and informative documents the capitularies, through which Charlemagne attempted to govern and to legislate for his vast and diverse realm, a considerable amount of miscellaneous information can be gleaned about Frankish military regulations at the beginning of the ninth century. Anticipating King Henry II of England by four hundred years, they prohibited the export of armor. In 807 it was decreed that all who held benefices were obligated to perform military service. Capitularies dated 804 and 811 required that every horseman should have a shield, lance, sword, dagger, bow, quiver, and arrows. Why the last three items were required is puzzling, because western Europeans never became proficient as horse archers. Other regulations provided that every man who possessed twelve *mansi* (a land measure of unknown dimensions, about as precise as the Old English *hida*) must have a mail shirt, and that when called out for active duty, each soldier should bring rations for three months and clothing for six. It is reasonable to infer that service for half a year could be exacted by the king.

At the same time, efforts were made to improve the quality of the infantry arm, as well as to afford some relief to the average free man, who must have been hard-pressed by reason of Charlemagne's almost annual campaigns.

While every man in occupation of four *mansi* was required to serve in person, provisions were made to ease the burden of military service on the smaller freeholders. These were to be grouped in combinations so that their holdings added up to four *mansi*—for example, 3 and 1; 2 and 2; 1, 1, and 2. One individual of the group was to be designated to render the service due from all four *mansi*. This reform of 808 undoubtedly improved the Frankish infantry, but unlike the somewhat similar five-hide system in England, it narrowed the limits within which military service was confined. It seems likely that the man with military experience was selected repeatedly to serve on campaign, and gradually he became lord over those who tended his fields while he was away at the wars. In this sense, Charlemagne's effort to improve the efficiency of the infantry was but another step in the development of feudalism. The capitularies also show that some attempts were made to provide the basic essentials of a commissariat and a supply service. The military train was to consist of carts carrying stores of flour, wine, and pork. In addition, it was specified that mills—presumably hand mills for grinding grain—should be carried, as well as pioneer tools such as adzes, shovels, axes, planes, augers, and slings. The extent to which these decrees were implemented is, unfortunately, unknown. Finally, the great Frankish monarch laid down rules designed to enforce some degree of discipline. A capitulary of 801 prescribed that desertion should be punished by confiscation of property, or by death if it occurred under special circumstances. In 811 he ruled that men convicted of drunkenness should be placed on a water diet until the offense was acknowledged. Admittedly this information is sketchy at best, but details of this nature are available for no other western military organization of the period.

Charlemagne, of course, never developed a regular permanent army. The granting of benefices to men who would agree to perform military service had to be watched carefully by monarchs who desired to check decentralizing trends. Indeed, the very survival of the Carolingian state depended on its ability to retain the upper hand. Strong control was required over the benefice holders to insure that the promised service was rendered or, if it was not, that the benefice was recalled and granted to someone who would honor the obligation. It had to be decreed that a beneficed landholder who failed to meet his military obligation should be punished by the confiscation of his estates. Government officials also had to be closely watched lest they use their benefices to advance their personal interests rather than those of the state. Most important, care had to be exercised to prevent the handing down of official position and benefice together in the same family. The strong Carolingians did these things well, but they could do no more than hold feudal tendencies in check. Once the heavy hand of Charlemagne was removed, they were accelerated.

While the trend was probably irreversible, its acceleration was due primarily to two factors. The first was the long and bitter civil wars among the descendants of Charlemagne which virtually destroyed the Carolingian state. The shadowy emperors and kings who flit across the pages of ninth- and tenth-century chronicles had neither the ability nor the authority to prevent the growth of great feudal estates and the concomitant growth of private armies. Military power thus became localized in the armies of wealthy and powerful lords, both lay and ecclesiastical, who hastened to create benefices from their own lands on which to quarter fighting men. This only served to strengthen the association of military service, vassalage, and landholding, and the tradition soon became established that only a vassal might fight on horseback. As has been so aptly stated, "The new system also brought into the ranks of the landed nobility a host of upstart adventurers, whose chief title to nobility . . . was that they rode a noble beast, the horse." [2]

The armies of Frankish monarchs no longer consisted of the general levy of all free men, each under the banner of the king's deputy, the count, but of the mounted contingents of vassals commanded by powerful nobles. Finally, Charles the Bald, king of the West Franks (840–877), decreed that every man who had a horse, or ought to have one, should come mounted to the host. As early as 847, the three grandsons of Charlemagne had declared that every free man must have a lord; and the fact that benefices had become heritable property must have had *de facto* recognition long before Charles the Bald gave it official sanction by the Capitulary of Kiersey (Quiercy), in 877. When every man had to have a lord, when every official was a landholder, when every holder of a benefice had to serve as a mounted soldier, and when offices, benefices, and military obligations became hereditary, feudalism was complete, at least in practice.

At the same time there was a significant change in terminology. The word *feudum* (fief, fee), of Germanic

[2] James Westfall Thompson and Edgar Nathaniel Johnson, *An Introduction to Medieval Europe, 300–1500* (New York, 1937), pp. 297–298.

origin, gradually replaced the Latin *beneficium*. In short, the fief was the benefice become hereditary. Everywhere smaller landholders placed themselves and their vassals under the protection of a more powerful lord, and north of the Loire, virtually all land was brought into the feudal relationship. Elsewhere—in southern France, in Germany, and in Italy—the persistence of allodial tenure, land that was held of no lord, prevented the significant extension of feudal holdings for centuries, but in the heart of the old Carolingian state—in the Rhineland and northern France—feudalism, the decentralization of political and military power, predominated.

To the political anarchy of the ninth and tenth centuries was added a second factor: the appearance of new barbarian enemies—the Vikings and the Magyars, or Hungarians. The impact of the Magyars and their influence on the development of German feudalism is discussed in a later chapter. For Europe west of the Rhine the Viking invasions had a more important effect on the evolution of military concepts. The causes of the Norse invasions are a subject for controversy even among specialists, and no attempt is made to deal with them here. But for whatever reasons, large numbers of barbarian raiders emerged from the misty north in the waning years of the eighth century, and for the next two centuries western Europe was to know only brief surcease from their attacks. Although England was the first land to experience Viking raids (784), the Anglo-Saxons never found it necessary to do more than modify an existing and effective military system. At first the Norsemen seem to have been interested primarily in trade, but this they soon abandoned for the more profitable profession of piracy. Each spring the

Vikings would appear in their admirably constructed long ships; they would land on the coast or sail up some river to sack and burn a town or abbey, and then they would depart with their booty. Considering the mobility of the Vikings, their control of the sea lanes, and the impossibility of predicting where and when the next strike might come, even an efficient government would have had problems in organizing an adequate defense. However, as long as imperial defenses held up at all, the Norse raids were little more than a bearable nuisance. But with the beginning of the civil wars late in the reign of Louis I (Louis the Pious, 814–840), the Vikings were not slow to take advantage of the opportunity offered by the collapse of Carolingian authority. A mere enumeration of towns sacked or assaulted between 840 and 885 is indicative of the initiative of the invaders as well as of the ineffectiveness of the later Carolingians: Rouen, Tours, Orléans, Paris, Amiens, Aachen, Cologne, Nîmes, and Avignon. Not until the successful defense of Paris in 885–886 was there a definite break in the almost uniform and dismal record of Viking successes.

As the vulnerability of the Frankish empire became more apparent, the Norsemen became bolder in their enterprises. Instead of confining their activities to hit-and-run raids, they soon began to beach their ships in a convenient location, fortify the position with bank-and-ditch earthworks, and leave a garrison to hold the bridgehead. The remainder of the company would commandeer all the horses in the neighborhood and set off on a cross-country raid. The problem of how to deal with the horsed Vikings was one with which the quarreling descendants of Charlemagne could not begin to cope. The local infantry levies were utterly helpless against the highly mobile raiding columns which could strike at a time and place of their own choosing. Thus the necessity of working out some method to counter the mobility of the Norsemen gave further impetus to the feudalization of military service and lent further importance to the role of the mounted warrior.

Although a good deal can be pieced together about the nature of Carolingian military institutions and the transition from infantry to mounted service, very little can be gleaned from the annals and chronicles about how the troops were utilized. For example, along the borders of the Frankish empire, Charlemagne and his successors established frontier counties known as marks, or marches. These were military districts in which the chief official, the *Markgraf*, or count of the march, exercising palatine (independent) jurisdiction, was responsible for defending the frontier against the attacks of barbarians or Moslems. But of the nature and number of the forces at the disposal of the *Markgraf* nothing is known except that in some areas the system of military benefices was extended to newly conquered districts. Because of the Viking threat, marches were later established even in such interior regions as the Ile de France.

Perhaps the best description of Frankish methods of warfare during the Carolingian period is to be found in the *Tactica* of the Byzantine emperor Leo VI (Leo the Wise, 886–912). This military treatise, written about 900, contains a chapter outlining the tactics of the various enemies with whom Byzantine generals had to deal and suggesting the best methods of coping with them. Leo noted that the Franks of his day were bold, daring, proud to a fault, and willing to fight whenever battle was offered, and that they regarded any movement to the rear as disgraceful. If the emperor's assessment is at all correct, the Franks at the beginning of the tenth century committed all the military errors which modern writers are prone to associate with feudal warfare. They were undisciplined and disorderly; a Frankish column on the march apparently resembled a large-scale outing, with no guards out and no proper reconnaissance of the country through which it was advancing. This made the column especially vulnerable to attacks from the flanks and rear. Camp was made casually; thus a bivouac was an easy prey to night attack, and it was easy to draw the Franks into an ambush by a feigned flight. On the other hand, the charge of the Frankish knights was to be avoided if at all possible, for the weight of the mailed northerners could sweep away anything unfortunate enough to be caught in its path. It should be noted in passing that this tactical advantage was a constant factor in the wars of the feudal period; Turks, Moors, Byzantines, and Egyptians—all the external enemies faced by Europeans—feared the charge of the heavy feudal horse. Man for man and horse for horse, they were no match for the westerners, and they sought by all sorts of tactical expedients to nullify this preponderance in weight. As feudal commanders became more sophisticated, they sought, in turn, to create tactical situations in which the charge of the armored knights would be decisive. Although at first Byzantine commanders with their professional battalions and brigades were able by ruse and strategem to defeat the wild, undisciplined rushes of

Frankish armies, by the end of the eleventh century they were experiencing considerable difficulty with the Normans of southern Italy.

It is important to remember, however, that during the tenth century, most of the Frankish engagements which have been recorded were fought between opponents of roughly equal military skills. Unfortunately, the notation is all that has survived in most instances. The celebrated action at Roncesvalles in 778 was militarily unimportant. The rear guard of the Frankish army was ambushed and defeated by the Basques in the Pyrenean pass of Roncesvalles—a dismal conclusion to Charlemagne's disappointing campaign into northern Spain. It is noteworthy, however, because it furnished the inspiration for the greatest of the medieval epics, the *Song of Roland,* in many respects the very mirror of the chivalric ideal. An imposing list of battles fought during the Carolingian period can be compiled, but very little is known of the size and composition of the armies involved or of the tactics employed by the contending forces. It is also likely that the actions described in most detail were exceptional, rather than routine, encounters. This is certainly the case with Abbo's account of the great Viking siege of Paris in 885–886, *Bella Parisiacae Urbis.* The city had twice been captured and sacked by the Norsemen, but in 885 the conduct of the defense had been entrusted to a Count Odo, whose heroic and successful efforts in repelling the determined onslaughts of the attackers—it may be doubted that, as Abbo says, they had forty thousand men and seven hundred ships—led to his elevation to the throne of the West Franks three years later.

Another example is the well-planned campaign of 801–

802, which was commanded by Charlemagne's son Louis. The invasion of Catalonia had for its objective the reduction of Barcelona: because it must have been thought certain that the Moors would react strongly to a threat to so important a city, precautions had to be taken against Moslem attempts to interfere with siege operations. Louis, who commanded a mixed army of Franks, Provençals, Aquitanians, Gascons, and Goths, accordingly divided his force into three corps, one of which at once began the siege of Barcelona. A second corps under the command of Count William of Toulouse was posted as a covering force some miles west of the city, the direction from which a relieving army seemed most likely to approach. Louis, with the third division, stationed himself nearer Roussillon, his base of operations, a position from which he might readily dispatch assistance to either of his other corps if necessary. An attempt was made to relieve Barcelona by the emir of Córdoba, Hakam (796–822), who marched by way of Saragossa. But he did not attempt to dislodge the covering force of Count William from the strong position in which it had been posted. As soon as Hakam had withdrawn, Count William's corps joined the troops before Barcelona; winter quarters were constructed with lines of circumvallation and contravallation drawn about the city and the besieging force. The investment continued throughout the winter, until the Moorish garrison was starved into surrender. Although Charlemagne had on occasion conducted winter operations against the Saxons, a campaign such as that of 801–802 must have been truly exceptional both in magnitude and duration, which doubtless accounts for the fuller notice accorded it.

Similarly, the disaster which befell a Frankish army on

the banks of the Weser in 782 may also be regarded as exceptional. During one of the many campaigns required to conquer the Saxons, a force recruited in Thuringia and Franconia, commanded by two counts, Geilo and Adalgis, was marching to meet the hostile tribesmen. From another direction a second Frankish column, under the command of a Count Theuderich, was also converging on the Saxons. Anticipating an easy victory, which they did not wish to share with Theuderich, Geilo and Adalgis urged their men forward as fast as their horses would carry them. As a result the column lost its formation and engaged the Saxons, drawn up in front of their camp, in piecemeal fashion. The haphazard attack was easily beaten off, and four counts and two *misi dominici* (royal agents), as well as more than a score of additional men of high position were slain. Among the rank and file the slaughter was correspondingly great. Of infantry participation not a word is said. Two explanations come immediately to mind. It seems a bit early in the evolution of the Frankish army for a column to be composed of cavalry only, but the possibility can by no means be ruled out. It seems more likely, however, that infantry are not mentioned because they were so far outdistanced by the overeager cavalry that they never got into the fight. This would also help to explain the apparent ease with which the Saxons beat off the disordered attack of the Frankish horse.

Equally unusual was the victory gained by the East Frankish King Arnulf over a Viking host at Louvain in 891. After a successful raid through Austrasia, the heartland of the old Frankish state, the Norse army returned to its fortified camp at Louvain. This base was located in a loop of the river Dyle, with a ditch and a bank that was topped by a palisade thrown across the open end of the loop. It was a formidable position, difficult to attack because of the marshy approaches to the defenses. Nevertheless, King Arnulf was determined to attack it. He ordered his troops to dismount, a measure which the chroniclers mentioned as unusual, because the Franks were not accustomed to fight on foot. The comment is indicative of the degree to which the Franks had become a nation of mounted warriors since the time of Charlemagne, a century earlier. With the king leading the way, the Frankish army slogged through the marsh, scrambled across the ditch, and began to hack away at the palisades with their swords. A breach was eventually made, and although the Vikings offered fierce resistance within the camp, their shield wall was finally broken, and thousands of Norsemen are said to have been driven into the Dyle and drowned. This is one of the few instances in which a Viking camp was carried by storm, and it had the double effect of raising the morale of the East Franks and of inducing caution in the Norse command. After Arnulf's victory, the East Frankish realm was singularly free of major Viking raids.

Although almost nothing is known of the "typical" Frankish order of battle after mounted service became normal in the tenth century, it is possible to speak with more assurance about the arms and equipment of the individual warrior. His protective gear consisted of a conical steel cap, usually with a nasal bar to protect his face from sword cuts. Somewhat later a mail panel was attached to protect the back of the neck. No further improvement was made until the end of the twelfth century, when the so-called pot helm, a more or less cylindrical steel helmet with eye slits and perforations to facilitate breathing, was introduced. This was not an unmixed blessing, for until a method was devised to secure it firmly to the body armor, it was easily knocked askew, and the wearer could not see what he was about until he straightened it again. The *miles*, or knight of the early feudal period, also wore a short-sleeved, knee-length mail shirt and carried a large kite-shaped shield. These remained virtually unchanged until the twelfth century. Then the mail shirt began to lengthen its sleeves; the shirt split into leg coverings at the bottom, until finally the knight was encased in mail. As the body became more completely protected, the size of the shield diminished. As armor became heavier, it required a sturdier horse to carry the increased weight, and knightly equipment became more costly. For this among other reasons, by the second half of the twelfth century the records begin to refer to a second class of mounted soldier—the sergeant—whose equipment was, presumably, less complete or less elaborate than that of the *miles*.

Offensive armament consisted of a long cutting sword and a lance. Until the beginning of the twelfth century the lance seems to have been a versatile weapon. The Bayeux tapestry, which was probably embroidered in the early 1070's, suggests that it might be employed in any one of three ways. It could be hurled as a javelin, it could be thrust at an enemy with an overhand motion of the knight's arm, or it could be held between the rider's upper arm and body so that the blow imparted the total weight of the armored rider and his horse. It seems likely that the last use became standard before the middle of the twelfth century.

Infantry equipment was roughly similar to that of the mounted arm—steel cap with nasal, mail shirt, shield, sword, and lance. In England the use of the lethal two-handed Danish axe, so prominent at Hastings, persisted well into the twelfth century. At the battle of Lincoln in 1141 some, at least, of the Lincoln militia—Lincoln was part of the old Danelaw—were armed with this weapon, and King Stephen is reported to have used it to good effect after his sword broke.

During the Carolingian period another characteristic of feudal warfare first assumed importance. This was the castle, which is generally agreed to be a private or personal fortification of a king or member of the baronial class. It is distinguished from communal fortifications such as the *Burgen* built by Charlemagne, the later Carolingians, and the Saxon kings of Germany, and the burhs constructed by Alfred the Great and his successors in England. These were designed to afford protection to entire communities, especially on exposed frontiers. Castles, on the other hand, became common throughout most of western Europe and had as their main function the protection of the lord, his family, and the lord's garrison. Castles built by kings and garrisoned in their name were usually located to dominate important lines of communication such as roads, bridges and fords, and ports, to guard frontiers, or to provide centers of police and administrative authority. It is not possible to say when private, as opposed to public, fortifications began to appear, but by 864, Charles the Bald found it necessary in the Capitulary of Pistres to order that all private fortifications be destroyed, but there is nothing to show that the decree was enforced. While evidence is lacking to show that castles were numerous in the West Frankish state in the ninth century, an increasing number of references can be dated to the tenth and eleventh centuries.

North of the Loire, the first castles were what are technically referred to as "ring-works," consisting of a bank and ditch, probably palisaded, thrown around the residence of a private landholder. This pattern seems to have been common throughout western Europe, including England and the Rhineland in addition to northern France. The next important development in castle construction—the incorporation of a high mound of earth, the motte, within the ring-work—occurred toward the end of the tenth century in Anjou. From here it is alleged to have spread to other parts of France as the decentralization of public authority continued, and it was introduced elsewhere decades later as, for example, into England by the Norman favorites of Edward the Confessor.

This concept of the evolution of castle structure has been challenged, and perhaps all current interpretations will have to be re-examined in the light of new archeological evidence. It has been suggested that the motte was a comparatively late development—perhaps dating only from the Norman Conquest—and that from England it spread over western Europe. But whatever the origin, the motte-and-bailey (mount-and-court) castle was found almost everywhere feudalism took root, for obvious military reasons. Since timber was plentiful, such structures were easy to erect, and though they were vulnerable to fire, if resolutely defended they could usually hold out until relief was forthcoming from some neighboring stronghold. Stone castles were rare before the second half of the eleventh century because of their enormous cost, the tremendous amount of labor required for their construction, and a shortage of skilled workers.

The Carolingian era saw the crystallization of the insti-

tutions usually referred to as feudal. Some had their origin
in the distant Roman and Germanic past, but it was only
in the eighth century that they began to merge into the
distinct forms that characterize the feudal period. The
economic collapse resulting from the barbarian migra-
tions and the assaults of Islam, the incessant civil wars
among the descendants of Charlemagne, and the new
waves of barbarian assailants sapped the resources of a
government that was never much more than a German
tribal monarchy. A state which could neither pay its troops
nor provide their equipment had to find some method of
raising an army. The traditional infantry levy of all free
men was too unwieldy to contend effectively with fast-
moving Moors and Vikings. Out of the seeming chaos
of the eighth to the tenth century, military feudalism
emerged. The fighting man became a mounted warrior—
a knight, a chevalier, a *Ritter*. He held a parcel of land
on condition that he render mounted service to the lord
from whom he received the land. Military service thus became attached to the land rather than to the individual:
whoever held the land—the fief—was obligated to perform the service (*servitium debitum*). Just how this service was performed in the formative years is as yet un-
clear. Probably there was no limit, initially, to the length
of time a knight might be required to spend in the field.
Eventually, however, a fairly common standard of forty
days per year became fixed, although it seems likely that
in England, from the Conquest until sometime during the
middle years of the twelfth century, a tour of sixty days
could be demanded by the king. Details varied from place
to place. In England and Normandy, knight service was
closely associated with castle-guard duty; in Germany,

castle-guard was not even considered one of the knightly obligations.

As centralized military and political institutions gradually disappeared during the ninth and tenth centuries, the functions of government and defense were assumed or usurped by local magnates who granted fiefs to their followers and in effect created private armies which enabled dukes and counts to carry on basic public administrative and military functions. The castles of the magnates dominated the countryside, and little more than lip service was given to a distant and ineffective emperor or king.

From the lands north of the Loire where military feudalism evolved most completely, it spread in various ways through much of western Europe. By a process of imitation and assimilation, feudal institutions appeared in the Rhineland and southern Germany, in France south of the Loire, in Burgundy, and in the Christian kingdoms of Spain. By virtue of the Carolingian conquest, northern Italy was exposed to feudal influences, and in southern Italy, Sicily, and England, feudalism was imposed by Norman conquerors. Finally, in Syria and Palestine what is sometimes described as "the perfect feudal society" was established following the success of the First Crusade. It is necessary to keep in mind, however, that feudalism as an export was always modified to a greater or lesser extent by pre-existing conditions, and that feudalism in Germany, France, Spain, England, Italy, and Syria differed because of geographical, social, and institutional factors which antedated its introduction.

2

Military Feudalism and
the Early Capetians

To the casual student, feudal institutions—the lord-vassal relationship, fealty and homage, the military obligation attached to a piece of land—are usually associated with northern France, and with the first Capetian kings. Some writers, in a laudable effort to describe feudalism as simply as possible, give the impression of a certain institutional unity throughout the lands north of the Loire. It is necessary, however, to make important reservations, for even in northern France the development of feudal institutions was far from uniform. Celtic Brittany never developed a regular feudal hierarchy, and numerous counts struggled continuously for the empty title of duke. In Picardy, sandwiched between thoroughly feudalized Normandy and Flanders, allodial holdings were common well into the thirteenth century, and, except for castle-guard, obligatory military service was practically unknown. Similar institutions may be found in different regions, but the political and military conditions resulting therefrom were often dissimilar. North of the Loire the term "feudalism" applies to the relative order and stability of Normandy,

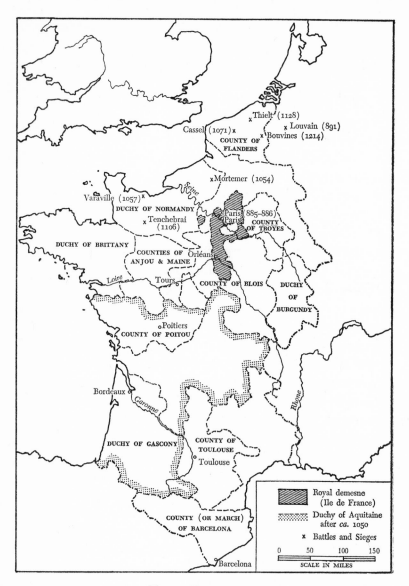

Thielt (1128) x
Louvain (891) x
Cassel (1071) x
Bouvines (1214) x
COUNTY OF
FLANDERS

Mortemer (1054) x

Seine

Varaville (1057) x
DUCHY OF NORMANDY
Tenchebrai x
(1106)
DUCHY OF BRITTANY

Paris (885–886)
Paris
COUNTY
OF TROYES

COUNTIES OF
ANJOU & MAINE
Orléans

Loire
Tours
COUNTY OF BLOIS
DUCHY
OF
BURGUNDY

Poitiers
COUNTY OF POITOU

Bordeaux
Garonne

Rhône

DUCHY OF GASCONY
COUNTY OF
TOULOUSE
Toulouse

COUNTY (OR MARCH)
OF BARCELONA

Barcelona

Royal demesne
(Ile de France)

Duchy of Aquitaine
after ca. 1050

x   Battles and Sieges

0   50   100   150

SCALE IN MILES

Map 1. France *ca.* 1035

Flanders, and Anjou, as well as to the anarchy that prevailed in the royal demesne until the time of Louis VI
(1108–1137).

The tenth century may be considered the period of
feudal consolidation. During this time all the advantages
seemed to lie with the great landed magnates who neglected no opportunity for self-aggrandizement. The inability of a central government to provide an adequate
defense against Viking attacks was excuse enough for the
raising and maintaining of private armies. The rivalry
between the Carolingians and the Capetians after 887 for
the throne of the West Franks, and the fact that the crown
remained elective enabled the great nobles to play off one
candidate against another and to extract the maximum in
concessions from the successful one. From the point of
view of the nobles, the situation could hardly have been
improved. Throughout the century they grabbed offices
and the lands of the royal fisc (those lands and rights from
which the king derived his revenues), never very extensive in the western part of the Carolingian empire, and
these they succeeded in making hereditary. The kings of
the West Franks were poor, even in the best of times, and
by the end of the tenth century, the royal demesne had
been reduced to little more than the city of Laon. The
only consistent support for a strong monarchy came from
the church, which suffered from the depredations and
usurpations of the lay nobility and strove to establish a
monarchy powerful enough to curb the activities of the
secular lords.

Such was the general situation when, in 987, the West
Frankish nobles and prelates elected Hugh, duke of
France, their king. Hugh was a considerable landholder

in the Ile de France, which was the center of his duchy; he was count of Orléans, Paris, and Dreux, as well as the immediate overlord of some fifteen other counties. Hugh was also head of the house of Capet, whose members had been rivals of the Carolingians for the past century. The lay and ecclesiastical electors, of course, had no intention of establishing a hereditary dynasty when they elected Hugh, but the new king had other ideas. On the ground that the burden of kingship was too great for one man to bear, he contrived to obtain the consent of the nobles to the association of his eldest son as coruler, thus beginning a practice which was continued by his successors. This scheme, together with the Capetian ability to produce male heirs, made the French crown hereditary.

To make clear the position of the first Capetians, it is necessary to say something about the three levels of authority on which they operated. First of all, they were the crowned and annointed kings of the West Franks (*reges francorum*, in contemporary terminology), and as such were the successors of the Carolingian monarchs. They were also the feudal overlords or suzerains of all the great vassals of the crown. Finally, and most important for the period under consideration, they were the rulers of their own duchy, the duchy of France—Paris and the country round about. This region was the nucleus of the Capetian demesne, since it included most of their fief.

As kings, Hugh and his successors enjoyed in theory all the traditional authority of their Carolingian predecessors. They could issue decrees that had the force of law everywhere in the kingdom. They could summon every able-bodied free man to their standard for military duty. Their officers—the counts—exercised jurisdiction thoughout the realm in the king's name. But most of the prerogatives of royalty were of little practical value to Hugh or to any of his successors until the second half of the twelfth century. If decrees were issued, the counts might or might not enforce them, depending on circumstances. Although they were the king's officers, the counts were hereditary officials, and the king was powerless to control them, let alone remove them from office. And the fighting men of the kingdom were, of course, the vassals of feudal lords to whom they were obligated for the performance of military service. About the only practical advantage derived from being king was that the monarch's person was sacrosanct, and even the most casehardened baron would think a long time before lifting a weapon against the person of the Lord's annointed. As the capstone of the feudal structure, the king could demand from the dukes, counts, archbishops, and bishops all the regular feudal services, including military service. In reality none of these rights amounted to very much. The dukes of Aquitaine did not recognize the Capetian dynasty for generations, and not until the twelfth century did the two greatest magnates of the Midi—the duke of Aquitaine and the count of Toulouse—even bother to do homage to a Capetian king. Even north of the Loire, the overlordship of the king was hedged about with reservations. While the duke of Normandy acknowledged his obligation to do homage and to attend the royal court, he also insisted that the king had to come to the frontiers of the duchy when these services were to be performed. Similarly, the great vassals of northern France admitted their suzerain's right to demand military service, but being shrewd bargainers, they compounded for contingents that were, as will be noted later, ridiculously small in comparison with their total military resources.

Thus whatever real power the early Capetians exercised was in their duchy of Paris. On the accession of King Hugh in 987, this became the royal demesne, and here he could exercise full powers of government. The vassals of the demesne could ignore their feudal obligations with less impunity than could the great feudatories, and the power of the Capetian king depended in large measure on the military resources of the demesne and the extent to which he could control these resources. Hugh and his successors could count on only one other source for reliable political and military support. At one time or another, Hugh's ancestors had controlled many more counties than he possessed at the time of his election. Some had been alienated to younger sons; others had been granted as fiefs to buy support. But in granting these lands, the Capetians had been very careful to retain control of the bishoprics, a matter of extreme importance. The lord or patron of an episcopal see controlled, in practice, the selection of the bishop. Bishops were also important barons who owed knight service to their patron. The Capetians, then, could assure themselves of trustworthy vassals on whom they could rely for military service.

It was fortunate for them that this was the case, for Hugh and his immediate successors were unable to maintain order in the royal demesne, limited though it was in extent. The petty lords of the Paris region, the barons of Montmorenci, Coucy, and Le Puiset, built strong castles from which they defied the authority of their duke and king with gusto. The first Capetians could not even travel from Paris to Orléans with any assurance of safety. They had to secure a safe-conduct from the lord of Le Puiset, whose castle at Etampes dominated the road between the two cities. Conditions in the Ile de France continued to deteriorate from the time of King Hugh down to the accession of Louis VI more than a century later. It is small wonder, under the circumstances, that the greater vassals of the crown treated their suzerain with scant respect. His military resources, compared to their own, were insignificant. When it suited the purpose of a great feudatory, he allied with the king against other lords; but he was just as willing, when it seemed to be profitable, to join a combination against his suzerain.

On the whole, however, the greater feudatories simply ignored the king. Their contributions to the feudal host, as has been noted earlier, bore no relation whatever to their military resources. The count of Champagne, who by the middle of the twelfth century had accumulated fiefs which enabled him to demand the service of 2,300 knights, discharged his military obligations to the crown by sending a contingent of ten knights. The count of Flanders, who could contract with the king of England to put a thousand heavy cavalry into the field in return for a money fief, was required to furnish a mere twenty knights to the royal host. Under certain circumstances—although here the evidence is admittedly conflicting—the duke of Normandy might fulfill his military obligation with ten knights, albeit his own vassals were responsible for the service of about 1,500. It would seem that the king was due no more than 500 to 700 knights, even if all the crown vassals honored their obligations, which must have been seldom, although there were notable exceptions.

The royal army on campaign must have conformed very

nearly to the popular and contemptuous concept of a "feudal levy." It must be noted, however, that the king's army was not drawn exclusively from feudal sources. He could, for the petty campaigns in the Ile de France, depend upon the knight service of those episcopal sees over which he retained control, plus the knightly quotas of those demesne tenants who were in the royal obedience at that particular moment. These slender contingents were augmented by the peasant levies from the church lands and from the king's own *villes* (peasant villages), units of doubtful military value. Altogether the royal host cannot have been impressive or very effective.

On rare occasions the king found it necessary or expedient to intervene in the affairs of one of the great fiefs. One incident occurred in 1071, during the reign of Philip I (1060–1108). In 1070, Count Baldwin VI of Flanders had been killed in battle, and the succession of his son, Arnulf III, was challenged by the late count's brother, Robert the Frisian. Arnulf appealed to his suzerain, the king of France, for aid. Philip responded with what may well have been close to the maximum force that he could put into the field. While the numbers are nowhere stated, twenty-seven feudal contingents are reported by contemporary chroniclers to have joined the king's standard for this campaign, which was conducted in the dead of winter. It should not be supposed, however, that Philip's army was exceptional in size. The contingent of the duchy of Normandy, under the command of the seneschal, William fitz Osbern, numbered exactly ten knights. Episcopal and demesne tenants figure prominently in the list, but although the combined armies of the king and Arnulf seem to have had a considerable numerical advantage

over the forces of Robert the Frisian, their fighting qualities were at best indifferent. In an engagement fought
near Cassel on 22 February 1071, Robert was completely
victorious. Arnulf III, a lad in his teens, and William fitz
Osbern, a veteran of the Norman occupation of England,
were slain in the action, and King Philip only halted his
flight from the field when he had reached Montreuil, some
forty miles distant. Even with the best of intentions, and
though he was at the head of the largest force he could
muster, the king could not protect a vassal in distress, and
it has been well said that the reign of Philip I marked the
nadir of Capetian fortunes. Although he was able to halt
the shrinking of the royal demesne and in fact to reverse
the trend, after so ineffective a regime there was nowhere
for the monarchy to go but up.

This was demonstrated by the reign of Philips's son
Louis VI, usually referred to as "the Fat." Louis was indeed overweight, and in his later years became so corpu-
lent that, like Brevet Lieutenant General Winfield Scott
(1786–1866), the conqueror of Mexico in 1847, he had
considerable trouble getting on a horse. But he had a more
realistic view of his position than had his predecessors.
Instead of wasting his limited resources in attempts to
assert vague and quite unenforceable claims over the great
feudatories, he set about the task of making himself master
of the petty tenants of the royal demesne. This in itself required exertions which must have taxed the energies of
the king. The principal obstacle to royal control was so
simple a construction as the motte-and-bailey castle. If
such a structure was seized, it was easy enough to pull
down the palisade and fill in the ditch. But once the
enemy had departed, it was almost equally easy to put it

together again. It is recorded that William the Conqueror had such a castle built at York in eight days.

Louis spent much of his time in petty wars that followed what came to be almost a stereotyped course. A vassal would be summoned, under safe-conduct, to appear before the royal *curia* to answer charges for some misdeed or atrocity. If he failed to appear, he was outlawed and excommunicated, and the king marched at once to lay siege to his castle. If the vassal appeared before the court and was condemned, he would openly revolt as soon as he reached the security of his castle. The king would act as he did before. He would take the field at the head of his troops and those of his ecclesiastical supporters and besiege the rebel in his castle. Sometimes the siege was unsuccessful. On occasion the rebels were strong enough to challenge and even defeat the king in the open field, but Louis kept up the pressure. It required three campaigns in seven years to secure the submission of Hugh, lord of Le Puiset, near Chartres, and Thomas de Marly defied his royal suzerain for fifteen years before he was finally trapped outside his castle of Coucy and mortally wounded. The other tenants of the demesne at last became aware that times were changing; they submitted to the king, and from the reign of Louis VI onward, they remained loyal vassals of the crown. Among them the Capetians found the constables and marshals who were their chief military officials.

But if Louis must be given most of the credit for putting the Capetian monarchy on a firm base, it was his able and thoroughly unpleasant grandson, Philip II Augustus (1180–1223), who established the supremacy of the crown over the great feudatories. Although Philip was never reputed to be a great soldier, on at least one occasion he proved himself to be a competent commander, as will be noted later. Philip's great contribution to the development of the military power of the French crown, however, like that of his older contemporary and rival, Henry II of England, lay in organization and in the use of stipendiary troops to make the state less dependent on the military resources of the nobility. By astute diplomacy and the judicious employment of military force, Philip was able to deprive King John of England of most of the fiefs that he held of the French crown and to increase the extent of the royal demesne by 400 per cent. Although something that, for want of a better term, may be called "neofeudalism" appeared during the Hundred Years' War, military feudalism in France, as in England, had become obsolescent by the end of the twelfth century.

The king could, of course, depend on the military service of his vassals and their contingents for only forty days a year. While some could be persuaded to extend their service—if they were paid for it—this expedient was not only uncertain; it did not adequately provide for the security of the realm during the long struggle with John of England and his allies. The towns also were obliged to furnish infantry contingents to the royal host for perhaps as long as three months per year. By instituting a tax resembling scutage, a money payment in lieu of military service, Philip enabled nobles, townsmen, and ecclesiastics to commute their military obligations to a money payment. The indications are that the baronage preferred to render service in person; the returns of 1202 show that only a small amount of money was paid by tenants in lieu of individual duty. On the other hand, although some towns continued to provide contingents—those of Corbie, Amiens, Beauvais, Compiègne, and Arras performed with credit at Bouvines in 1214—there was an increasing tendency for the communities to pay the tax rather than send troops.

With the money obtained from the towns and other sources, Philip Augustus raised what almost amounted to a permanent army made up of mercenaries. The employment of stipendiary troops was by no means an innovation in Capetian France. Duke William of Normandy hired them in large numbers for his attack on England in 1066, and his successors in Normandy continued to use them in their numerous wars. As early as 1138, Philip's father, Louis VII (1137–1180), had engaged the services of a mercenary band of 200 knights, archers, and crossbowmen. But by 1202, Philip II had in his employ a professional force estimated at from 2,700 to 2,800 men, of which about 2,000 were infantry, and 800 of other arms. The composition of this force is of some interest as an indication of growing specialization among mercenary troops. The evidence shows the presence of knights, mounted sergeants, mounted crossbowmen, foot sergeants (ordinary spearmen), foot crossbowmen and sappers among the troops receiving the king's pay. Most of them apparently served in castle garrisons, and although a comparative study has yet to be made, this would seem to be on a scale comparable to that of contemporary English monarchs. Equally interesting is evidence concerning the origin of these soldiers. The free lances of Brittany, Brabant, and the

Holy Roman Empire have quite possibly been overemphasized as a source of mercenary manpower. The French rolls of 1202 show that the knights, mounted sergeants, and crossbowmen all bore French names and that even the infantry captains were Frenchmen—implying at least that their commands were also French. By the time the military crisis of 1214 developed, with its threat of an attack on two fronts, Philip was able to muster some 24,000 to 27,000 men, divided into two field armies. Prince Louis with 800 knights, 2,000 mounted sergeants, and 7,000 infantry confronted King John in the south, while King Philip with 1,200 knights, 3,000 mounted sergeants, and perhaps 10,000 infantry faced the advance of Emperor Otto IV in northeastern France. A comparable military effort had probably not been seen in western Europe since William the Conqueror's assault on England more than a century and a half earlier.

When it comes to detailing actual military operations, the historian faces the same problem in dealing with Capetian France as he does in considering other areas—that of working the brief and often conflicting accounts of the chroniclers into something like a believable narrative. The battle of Cassel (22 February 1071) mentioned earlier in the chapter provides a rather extreme illustration. For an eleventh-century battle, it was given wide notice by contemporary and near-contemporary annalists, at least six of whom have provided details from which it ought to be possible to piece together a fairly accurate account of the action. Yet so vague is the Latin of the monkish writers and so conflicting are their stories of what happened, that the two principal modern authorities do not even agree on which of the contending armies held the castle of Cassel when the battle began.[1] With this caveat in mind, some of the military operations of the period will be examined.

Sieges of course played as important a role in the warfare of Capetian France as they did elsewhere in feudal Europe. Even in such relatively well-ordered states as Anjou and Normandy, rebellion was a common occurrence, and border raids were epidemic. Since rebels were seldom strong enough to challenge their suzerain in the open field, they usually took refuge in their castles, hoping to prolong resistance until the besieging army should break up of its own accord. Because at this time the defense enjoyed a considerable advantage over the attack, there was at least a chance that such passive resistance would be successful. The besieger had several possibilities open to him. Capture of a castle by storm was rather rare, but instances are known, as when Domfront was taken by assault in 1051. The besieger might also issue dire threats and warnings as to what would happen to the garrison if it continued to resist. These sometimes so intimidated the defenders that they surrendered the castle. The systematic devastation of the country around the castle—which the rebel could see from the walls of his stronghold—also occasionally produced the desired result. The castle of Le Mans was reduced by this method in 1063. But the surest way to effect a capture—though usually the most time-consuming—was to establish a close blockade and wait for hunger to do the work.

[1] See Augustin Fliche, *Le Règne de Philippe Ier, Roi de France* (1060–1108) (Paris, 1912), pp. 258–259; and Charles Verlinden, *Robert Ier, Comte de Flandre* (Paris, 1935), pp 66–68.

Siege warfare as it was practiced in the seventeenth and eighteenth centuries was virtually unknown. Medieval commanders seldom disposed of forces large enough to conduct a regular investment, and the best they usually could do was to establish strong, often fortified, posts outside the gates of a castle to prevent either egress or ingress. Only a commander who could hold his force together until the garrison had exhausted its food supply had much success in capturing a castle by this means.

Although sieges were quite numerous, pitched battles were comparatively rare, and the information about them is usually unsatisfactory. Some of the actions rise scarcely above the level of skirmishes, but in some the commanders showed considerable tactical skill, and in an instance or two there is even a hint of strategic insight. One such was the campaign of 1054, which culminated in the battle of Mortemer. King Henry I (1031–1060), at odds with the young Duke William of Normandy, decided to attack the lands of his recalcitrant vassal. Two columns invading Normandy from different directions were to push down the valley of the Seine on opposite sides of the river. The French main body, concentrated at Mantes under the command of King Henry, was to move down the west bank of the Seine. It was composed of the demesne tenants, as well as contingents from Berry, Sens, Blois, and Touraine, together with some Angevins possibly commanded by Count Geoffrey. The second column, which was to invade Normandy from the east, was under the command of the king's brother Eudes. It included contingents from the counties of Clermont and Ponthieu. This was a rather ambitious plan for the eleventh century, and Duke William was compelled to divide his available forces in order to keep the movements of the French invaders under observation. The duke took the responsibility of opposing the column commanded by King Henry, while Count Robert of Eu commanded the forces in eastern Normandy against Eudes. There is no way of estimating the numbers of any of the commands involved in the campaign.

Opportunity came first to the count of Eu. He observed that Eudes had allowed a large part of his column to disperse in search of plunder. With commendable dispatch he fell upon the remainder in the vicinity of Mortemer, not far from the eastern frontier of the duchy, and achieved complete surprise. As they became aware of the situation, the scattered French detachments hurried to the scene of the action, only to be defeated in detail. The French column was completely dispersed, with considerable loss, before it had penetrated more than fifteen miles inside the Norman frontier. So complete was the Norman victory that King Henry began a retreat as soon as he received news of the disaster. The battle of Mortemer can scarcely be listed among the major engagements of the eleventh century, but King Henry's plan was not without strategic merit, and Count Robert showed himself prompt to take advantage of the laxness of French discipline. He also seems to have been aware of the value of surprise.

The inability of the early Capetians to intervene effectively in the affairs of their great vassals was again demonstrated in August 1057. On this occasion King Henry I—he should at least be given credit for perseverance—allied with Count Geoffrey of Anjou to invade Normandy. Their army, whose size and composition are unknown, pushed northward in the general direction of Caen and Bayeux, although there is nothing to indicate that Henry and Geoffrey planned to attack either place. It may be assumed, from what followed, that the line of march lay to the west of the river Dives. Duke William concentrated his forces in the vicinity of Falaise, whence he cautiously followed the invaders, whose movements were reported to him by reconnaissance parties. His opportunity came when the invaders reached the neighborhood of Varaville, about ten miles northeast of Caen, and began to ford the Dives. The river at this point, however, is tidal, and before Henry and Geoffrey could get all their men across, the rising tide made the ford impassable. William at once swooped down upon the rear elements of the divided enemy army, inflicting such severe losses that Henry had no alternative to retiring from the duchy as hastily as possible. As he did in the campaign of 1054, the Norman commander took advantage of a favorable tactical situation to score an impressive victory. Duke William was serving a military apprenticeship, and the degree to which he had mastered the craft of generalship was to be demonstrated convincingly nine years later at Hastings.

Of less importance for the political and military destinies of France or Normandy was a skirmish which occurred near Bourgtheroulde in 1124. It has a place, however, in the history of tactical development in the Middle Ages. A band of Norman rebels commanded by Count Waleran of Mellent was at large, and the castellan of Evreux, Ralf of Bayeux, was assigned the mission of intercepting it. Drawing on the garrisons of neighboring castles, Ralf assembled about three hundred mercenary horse and forty archers who were mounted in some fashion so that they could keep up with the knights. Ralf and his men got astride the road on which the rebels were marching, and knowing that the latter must attempt to cut their way through, he prepared to meet the expected attack. He dismounted most of the knights and placed them squarely across Waleran's anticipated line of advance. The remainder were available to act as a reserve or to pursue a defeated enemy, since they retained their horses. The archers likewise dismounted and were posted on the left of the main position, but thrown forward at an angle so that they could fire into the flank of a column advancing along the road. The left was chosen because it would enable the archers to shoot at the unshielded right side of the enemy. All went as Ralf had planned. The rebels attempted to smash their way through the roadblock, with Count Waleran leading a charge of forty knights. The archers, aiming at the horses, brought almost all of them down, and the charge of a second squadron met the same fate. Ralf then ordered a general advance, and most of the surviving rebels were taken prisoner.

The skirmish near Bourgtheroulde is of interest for at least three reasons. First, and perhaps most important for an accurate assessment of the quality of military leadership in the twelfth century, it shows that even a minor officer could be relied upon to use troops with skill and imagination. Ralf and his professional soldiery accomplished their mission with what can only be characterized as professional *élan*. Next, this seems to be the first instance of putting archers on horseback so that they could keep up with the knights; it would be helpful to know whether it was a common practice or one the castellan of Evreux thought up for the occasion. Finally, Ralf's deployment of his troops is intriguing, since it presages the standard formation eventually adopted by English commanders operating against the French during the Hundred Years' War.

Of the pitched battles fought in France before the close of the twelfth century, only Tenchebrai (20 September 1106) and Thielt (21 June 1128) are of much military significance. Tenchebrai, the climax of the struggle for Normandy between Duke Robert and his brother King Henry I of England, is notable in several respects. Both sides brought large numbers of infantry into the field, and the king's army included English foot soldiers. Henry also utilized Breton mercenary horse, which were used to good advantage. He further devised an order of battle, quite sophisticated for the early twelfth century. A first line was formed of three bodies of Norman infantry: the men of Bayeux, commanded by Ralf of Bayeux; those of Avranches, under the direction of Robert of Mellent; and the levies of Coutances, under the command of William de Warenne. To each block of infantry were probably attached the knights from the same district, although their position with reference to the infantry is not known. Apparently there were about 700 mounted men in the first line. The king's second line consisted entirely of men on foot. To the Norman and English infantry Henry added a large number of dismounted knights to stiffen the formation. Here he posted himself where he could observe the action. Behind the second line, a tactical reserve was held to the number, it is said, of 700 knights—the number 700 appears with suspicious frequency in the accounts. On the extreme right, possibly out of sight of the battlefield, Henry stationed Count Hélie de la Flèche of Maine with his feudal horse, and the Breton mercenaries commanded by Count Alan, with a combined strength of about 1000 knights. This detachment had orders to strike in on the Norman left flank as soon as Duke Robert's troops were irrevocably committed to action. The two armies appear to have deployed about an equal number of infantry, but King Henry seems to have enjoyed better than a 3 to 1 superiority in mounted troops. This was the decisive factor. In the ensuing engagement, Duke Robert suffered a disastrous defeat and was taken prisoner, and King Henry became undisputed master of Normandy.

The fight near Thielt also involved a disputed fief of the French crown. After the murder of Count Charles the Good in 1127, King Louis VI attempted to extend royal influence into Flanders by supporting the claims of William Clito, the son of the dispossessed Duke Robert of Normandy. A majority of the Flemings supported the pretensions of Thierry of Alsace, whose relationship to the late count was closer than William's. After months of indecisive sparring, the armies of the two contenders met at Hackespol, near Thielt, on 21 June 1128. The order of battle was identical for each side: three divisions, lined up one behind the other—a fairly common medieval array which will be met with again in the discussion of Spain and Norman Italy. The only difference in the arrangements was that while Thierry had all his divisions in plain sight, William either by accident or design had his third division well to the rear and out of sight. William stationed himself with the advanced elements of his army; Thierry commanded the third, or reserve, division of his forces.

The action opened with a clash between the leading squadrons of the two armies, and soon the second division on each side had been committed, with neither having any marked advantage. Then Thierry, acting on the assumption that all of his enemy's forces were in action, threw in his reserve division for the clincher. The immediate result was that William's outmanned line began to give ground and soon appeared to be on the point of disintegration. But just at Thierry must have been congratulating himself on his apparent victory, the Clito's third division came crashing into the somewhat disordered and surely astonished ranks of the erstwhile victors. For some time the fighting raged indecisively, but William managed to rally a body of his broken first division, and its intervention decided the outcome. Thierry's army broke up, and the fugitives were pursued relentlessly by the victors. Had not William died later in the year, he might have established a line of Norman counts in Flanders as a result of his victory at Thielt.

Very little commentary is necessary in evaluating this engagement. It was unusual in that neither army seems to have contained any infantry. In spite of a generally accepted opinion, battles involving only mounted troops were most infrequent. The generalship was not particularly distinguished on either side, for it is not certain whether William's third division was deliberately concealed or whether it was simply late in getting on the field. The battle does, however, provide another proof of the dictum that the side which can commit the last reserve is the victor.

It is appropriate to close a discussion of field operations in Capetian France with some account of the campaign of 1214, which culminated in the battle of Bouvines. Although the battle itself was of great importance for the

history of England, France, and the Empire, the operations that preceded it are, perhaps, of even greater importance. They indicate how far western Europe had
moved from what can be termed "feudal localism" by the
beginning of the thirteenth century. The moving spirit behind the campaign was King John of England, who, even
his worst detractors admit, was not lacking in either diplomatic or military ability. He was intent on recovering the
lands that had been lost to Philip Augustus but was well
aware that his own resources were inadequate for so ambitious an undertaking. Increasingly, his English tenants-
in-chief were showing a reluctance to serve overseas at
their own expense. This was especially true after the loss
of Normandy, where many of them had held extensive
lands. John was therefore obliged to rely on the rather uncertain service of those French magnates still in Plantagenet obedience, on his mercenaries, and on his success
in building up a continental coalition to oppose Philip.
By playing upon the interests and jealousies of the princes
on France's eastern frontier and by dispensing money gen-
erously, John built up an impressive alliance which included his nephew, Emperor Otto IV; the dukes of Brabant, Limburg, and Lorraine; and the counts of Holland
and Namur. These dukes and counts were imperial vassals.
In addition, the coalition was joined by two of Philip's dis-
contented feudatories, the counts of Flanders and Bou-
logne.

The plan of campaign evolved by John was ambitious
in the extreme, and although this is not the first time in
medieval history that something like grand strategy can
be detected, it was certainly an advanced concept for the

early thirteenth century.[2] Instead of joining his allies in the Low Countries for a massive assault on northeastern France, the English king envisaged a double offensive which would put Philip between two fires. John was to undertake an invasion of Poitou and Anjou, in the Loire Valley, which would draw the French king southward to protect his recently won provinces. Meanwhile, the emperor with the princes of the Low Countries would concentrate in Flanders and march directly on Paris.

Accordingly, King John sailed from Portsmouth in February, disembarking at La Rochelle on the fifteenth with an army composed largely of stipendiary troops. The levies of Guienne were summoned, and the king marched into Poitou. Here he was joined by the counts of La Marche and Nevers, and together they overran the county in March. The column then invaded Anjou and crossed the Loire, producing the reaction from King Philip that John had expected. The feudal host was summoned, the contingents of the towns were mustered, and mercenaries were drawn from the regular garrisons. Marching by way of Saumur and Chinon, Philip, accompanied by his son Louis, attempted to get astride of John's line of retreat to Aquitaine. The English monarch, whose intelligence sources seem to have served him well, withdrew south of the Loire, evaded the French, and by 3 April was at Limoges. Thus far, John had carried out his part of the campaign brilliantly, and the French field army had been drawn far to the south.

Unfortunately for the campaign, John's allies were not

[2] Charles Oman, *A History of the Art of War in the Middle Ages* (2 vols.; 2d ed.; London, 1924), I, 468.

prepared to move at so early a date; their lack of preparation proved to be the salvation of the French king. Philip decided not to follow John into Guienne, and after punishing the districts in Poitou which had supported the invader, he marched eastward. Halting at Châteauroux, in Auvergne, Philip divided his command. An army of observation under the command of Prince Louis was detached to watch King John, and with the larger part of the field army the king recrossed the Loire and headed north. Furious as John must have been to get no word of the advance of his allies, he did not let his wrath interfere with his strategy. As soon as he learned of the king's retirement, he launched another offensive. In May he was again in Poitou; he crossed the Loire, and after accepting the submission of many Angevin towns, he invested the strong fortress of La Roche-au-Moine on 19 June. Prince Louis, unwilling to let such an important castle fall to the enemy, put his command in motion for its relief. To the approximately 10,000 troops assigned to Louis were added numerous local levies, which increased the strength, if not the efficiency, of his army. For his part, John had no great confidence in his Poitevin contingents, so he decided not to risk a battle. After an investment of fifteen days, he destroyed his siege engines before La Roche and recrossed the Loire on 3 July. Louis pursued the retreating enemy as far as Thouars, mauling John's rear guard in the process, and then returned to Anjou.

This ended operations in the Loire region, but the English king had done more than might reasonably have been expected, and he had done it very well. For four months he had kept large numbers of French troops tied up in the Loire Valley, away from the expected major offensive, without having to commit his unreliable troops to a major action. Whatever may be said of King John, his conduct of this campaign is above criticism.

As much cannot be said for the generalship of John's principal ally, Otto IV. He did not reach Aachen until 23 March, by which time John was already operating in Poitou. Otto dawdled here while collecting additional troops, and on 19 May, when John was already engaged in his second foray into Poitou, the emperor was still in Aachen celebrating the marriage of his daughter to the duke of Brabant. Only in June did he begin his march westward; not until 12 July did he get as far as Nivelles, in Brabant; and by about 20 July he was no farther than Valenciennes, in Hainaut. This was more than two weeks after John had retired south of the Loire, and any chance for effective cooperation had passed. It is not necessary to discuss the remainder of the campaign in detail.

At Bouvines (27 July 1214) King Philip won the signal victory of his reign in a hard-fought battle over the army of the emperor and his allies, but by no stretch of the imagination can it be considered a feudal battle. True, feudal elements participated, but an entire wing of the imperial army was composed of mercenaries, and infantry on each side played an important role.

It is necessary to point out the reasons for the failure of John's brilliantly conceived strategy. Timing was, of course, the essential factor in the execution of his plans. It was necessary for Otto to move while Philip was engaged with the English diversion in the Loire Valley. Although distance and poor communications undoubtedly played a part in the failure of the two commanders to coordinate their movements, there is also the suspicion that the emperor simply did not understand the importance of moving promptly. At Bouvines, neither Otto nor Philip showed as much skill in handling troops as Henry I had exhibited at Tenchebrai more than a century earlier. It is hard to escape the conclusion that the campaign of 1214 showed John to be more progressive in outlook than either his ally Otto IV or his antagonist Philip II. Edward IV (1461–1483) was not the first English general to appreciate the value of time in warfare.

Military developments in Capetian, or "feudal," France followed no consistent pattern. Here, in what is uniformly regarded as the cradle of feudalism, political and military disintegration reached a level to be found elsewhere during this period only in northern Italy, which, as will be noted later, was never completely feudalized. Such influence as the first Capetians exercised was wielded north of the Loire, and even here it was closely circumscribed. During the century of rivalry between the Carolingians and the Capetians, the great vassals were slowly but surely arrogating to themselves the civil and military powers that once pertained to the monarchy. The dukes of Normandy and the counts of Flanders, Champagne, and Anjou made their own the military vassals who had once owed service to the king. By the end of the tenth century, the great feudatories exercised effective military power, and the Capetian king, for all his theoretical authority, was finding it increasingly difficult to control the petty lords within the limited confines of the royal demesne. Very nearly two centuries elapsed before a Capetian king commanded enough military strength to compel recognition of his authority throughout the kingdom.

During this period fighting was almost continuous, as

kings, dukes, and counts sought to impose their will on unruly vassals and the vassals fought to retain their independence in order to do almost as they pleased. Exponents of "law and order" would have had a rough time in Capetian France, for even in the best-run states, crime and violence were almost a way of life for the feudal classes. But though wars and rebellions were common occurrences, battles were few and seldom of any great importance. "Castle warfare" was the usual form, with the weaker side taking refuge in its fortresses and hoping for the best. By the middle of the twelfth century the stone castles that add such a picturesque touch to the French landscape were beginning to appear in greater numbers, but only the wealthier magnates could afford them. In an earlier and more primitive age, even a simple knight, if he had enough peasant labor available, could build a motte-and-bailey castle of earth and timber that was as strong as those of greater lords who might possess half a dozen, and warfare tended to degenerate into interminable siege operations in all the lands north of the Loire.

Of the pitched battles, none had important political consequences save the action at Val-es-Dunes (1047), in which the intervention of King Henry I preserved the throne of Normandy for the young Duke William. So little is known of this battle that no attempt has been made to discuss it in this chapter. It was apparently a cavalry action—no infantry is mentioned at any rate—in which hard fighting rather than skillful generalship decided the day. The actions described, however, are of interest to the student of tactical history. They show, for one thing, that eleventh- and twelfth-century generals were capable of more than leading a simple cavalry charge. The reactions of Robert of Eu at Mortemer in 1054 and of Duke William at Varaville three years later show that commanders could be prompt to take advantage of opportunities that chance had put in their way. The sophisticated order of battle employed by Henry I of England at Tenchebrai in 1106, with its provision for a reserve and an unusual flanking detachment, is indicative of the range of tactical expedients utilized by feudal commanders. It seems safe to conclude that eleventh- and twelfth-century generals were adequate tacticians. There is even a hint of strategic insight in the French invasion of Normandy in 1054.

Even in that part of Europe—northern France—where feudalism conditioned military institutions more thoroughly than elsewhere—more than in Frankish Syria— there was never complete reliance on feudal resources and mounted combat. Infantry was rarely absent from the battlefield. On other occasions, as at Tenchebrai, the knights, or a portion of them, dismounted and fought on foot. In at least one instance, at Bergtheroulde, archers who rode to battle and dismounted to fight were used to good effect.

Mercenaries of various kinds are referred to at an early date, and they became an increasingly important factor in the military formula throughout the eleventh and twelfth centuries. The reforms of Philip II were based on the commutation of personal service for a money payment which enabled the crown to maintain a permanent nucleus of stipendiary troops. In peacetime these paid soldiers served in the garrisons of royal castles; when war broke out, they formed the hard core of the king's army.

By the beginning of the thirteenth century, the king of France was able to fight a war on two fronts to a successful conclusion, although this was, perhaps, due as much to the inability of his enemies to coordinate their movements as to anything else. The significant point is that Philip had made it possible for France to keep two armies in the field at the same time. As late as 1173, when the justiciar of England, Richard de Lucy, was investing a rebel garrison in Leicester, it was necessary to raise the siege and march northward when King William of Scotland invaded Northumberland. Even the England of Henry II could not maintain two field armies.

To summarize: Reliance on feudal military manpower was becoming obsolescent in the Capetian monarchy by the end of the twelfth century. Commanders showed ability to use the various arms either singly or in combination with considerable effectiveness. There appears to be little basis for the conventional view that in the feudal age mounted troops were the sole arbiter of battle or that feudal generals were incapable of working out appropriate tactical plans and combinations.

3

Warfare in
Norman Italy

The scope of this book does not permit a detailed examination of the incredible complexity of politics in the southern third of the Italian peninsula at the beginning of the eleventh century. It is, however, necessary to say something about them in order that the Norman conquest of this strategically important area can be seen in proper perspective. In many respects, the establishment of Norman dominion in southern Italy and Sicily is much more remarkable than the conquest of England half a century later. Duke William in 1066 had behind him the resources of one of the best-organized feudal states in western Europe, as well as the support of the reforming papacy, which, in those days, was of no mean value. The Norman adventurers in Italy—perhaps "freebooters" would be a more accurate term—who wrested the land from Lombard, Byzantine, and Moslem hands had little besides their own individual abilities and skill at swordplay to support them.

In the early years of the eleventh century, political rivalries and claims in southern Italy had resulted in al-

Map 2. Italy *ca.* 1100. Members of the Lombard League (1167) are shown in boldface.

most complete anarchy. Frontiers and alliances were constantly shifting. No modern authorities agree on what the actual situation was at any particular time; the surviving contemporary sources are invariably biased and at odds with one another; and even a reasonably accurate narrative of events is not easily constructed. One fact does emerge, however; it was the ruthless intelligence and military ability of a handful of Norman mercenaries that enabled them to profit from the confusion which reigned in southern Italy and to establish one of the strongest feudal states in Europe. But the application of the term "feudal" must be qualified here as elsewhere; the Norman genius for political and military organization put together a system which, combining Norman, Lombard, Byzantine, and Moslem elements, was able to withstand local insurrection and intervention by emperors and popes. Feudal elements were important in this system to be sure, but the Norman dukes of Apulia and the counts—later, kings—of Sicily would have been hard-pressed to maintain their positions with feudal military resources alone.

At the beginning of the eleventh century Sicily was in Moslem hands, divided among a number of virtually independent emirs. Until the second half of the century it was outside the range of Norman operations, so it requires no further discussion at this point. The heel and the toe of the Italian boot were subject to Byzantine jurisdiction. Apulia (the heel) and Calabria (the toe) formed the theme (administrative division) of Langobardia, governed by a Byzantine official known as the catapan. The catapan exercised supreme civil and military jurisdiction within the theme; thus he commanded the garrison troops, the militia furnished by the towns, and whatever reinforcements the government at Constantinople might see fit to dispatch in times of crisis. The theme was divided into provinces, each headed by a *turmarch*—also both civil governor and military commander—who was responsible to the catapan, whose headquarters were at Bari, on the Adriatic coast. The imposition of military and naval service bore heavily on the towns and produced revolts in 929 and again in 1009. The inhabitants of the theme, partly of Lombard extraction, found aid and comfort in the Lombard duchies which lay to the north and west of Langobardia.

There were three of these duchies, successor states to the old Lombard duchy of Benevento, which had disintegrated during the course of the ninth century. They were continually at odds with one another, with the Byzantines of Langobardia, and with the maritime city-republics of the west coast. On the west coast of the peninsula, north of Calabria, lay the principality, or duchy, of Salerno; also on the western slopes of the Apennines, but separated from Salerno by the territories of Naples, was the principality of Capua. Its short stretch of coastline on the Tyrrhenian Sea contained no significant ports. East of Capua and north of Salerno and Byzantine Apulia lay the duchy of Benevento, which straddled the Apennines. It had considerable frontage on the Adriatic, with a port at Siponto, and the celebrated shrine of St. Michael on Monte Gargano. In addition, there were three maritime city-states of some importance on the west coast—Amalfi, Naples, and Gaëta—which enjoyed considerable commercial prosperity during the tenth century. These cities usually acknowledged Byzantine supremacy, but to all intents and purposes they were independent.

Little is known about the military resources available to the authorities of these varied political entities. The garrison troops in Langobardia were, of course, units of the Byzantine imperial army, professionally organized, equipped, and led, but they cannot have been numerous. The military needs of the empire on the Balkan and Syrian fronts during the last half of the tenth century must have served to keep the Italian garrisons at a minimum level. The *militiae* of the towns, probably infantry levies, were apparently not considered very reliable, because a significant part of the population, Lombard in origin, tended to look for aid, in times of rebellion, to the independent Lombard dukes. These magnates were more than willing to support insurrections against the authority of Constantinople. In the Lombard duchies the principle of hereditary succession had been established. All offices remained within the gift of the prince, and feudalism had made no impression on the structure of society. Although in an earlier age the Lombards were respected, even feared, for their warlike character, by the tenth century they had long since ceased to count for much in the military annals of Europe. Because military service was compulsory, the dukes were provided with a militia of townsmen, but no mention is made of the Lombard aristocracy which figures so prominently in the wars of the eighth and ninth centuries.

A factor which greatly influenced the character of warfare in southern Italy was the existence of a large number of walled towns. These were not the rude palisaded communities of western and northern Europe; the walls of towns and citadels in lower Italy were stone walls which required for their reduction more sophisticated siege techniques than were in general use elsewhere. The maritime cities, naturally enough, relied on their fleets for protection. Only in Naples is there mention of land forces. Here the hereditary duke also held the title *magister militum* (master of the troops). As such he was commander of the armed forces of the city, which consisted of a rather numerous class of *milites* who had lands and privileges in the city and the surrounding countryside. The basic military weakness of the states in southern Italy was without doubt responsible for the appearance of the Normans in that part of the peninsula.

In 1009 a revolt against Byzantine rule began in Bari. The rebels, according to custom, quickly entered into an alliance with Gaimar IV of Salerno, Pandulf III of Benevento, and Pandulf III of Capua (these are two separate individuals). However, the combined forces of the Apulian rebels and the Lombard dukes were no match for the Byzantine professionals. In 1010, Bari was recovered by the catapan Basil, and the leader of the revolt, a certain Melus, fled into exile. He returned to southern Italy in 1015, and late in the year he happened to visit the shrine of St. Michael on Monte Gargano at the same time that a band of forty Normans, returning from a pilgrimage to Jerusalem, had stopped to worship. Melus sought the aid of the Normans in behalf of the Apulian insurgents. Apparently the pilgrims returned home as unofficial recruiting agents for the rebel leader. At any rate, it was not long before the first bands of Normans began to cross the Alps, the vanguard of adventurers and fortune seekers who for the next half-century filtered down into lower Italy. They were usually landless warriors, often the younger sons of minor tenants whose fiefs were too small to provide for numerous offspring. They brought nothing with them except their arms and horses, a willingness to fight, and the Norman genius for making the most of any opportunity.

The arrival of the first Normans was welcomed by the Apulian insurgents, whose forces consisted chiefly of foot levies from the towns. The Lombard dukes also recruited Norman mercenaries for their armies. The acquisition of cavalry units would add striking power to the none too steady contingents furnished by the towns. By 1017 the Apulian rebel Melus felt strong enough to resume active operations, and at the year's end he was in control of all Apulia from the river Fortore to Trani. But his success was short-lived. In 1018 the catapan Bojoannes took the field against the rebels, his army strengthened by detachments from the famed Varangian Guard. He encountered the enemy on the banks of the Otranto, and at Cannae he decisively defeated the rebels and virtually annihilated the Norman contingent. Only 10 of 250 Normans are said to have escaped from the field. For all practical purposes this ended the rebellion, at least for a time, and the Normans entered the service of the Byzantines, being posted to garrison fortresses on the frontier with Benevento. In spite of the catastrophe at Cannae, bidding for the services of Norman mercenaries seems to have been quite spirited, and during the following decade they were to be found in the armies of Salerno, Capua, and Naples as well as that of the catapan of Langobardia. They were still landless men, living by their swords, and were often ranged against each other in the petty wars of lower Italy.

In 1030, however, an incident occurred which was to alter the status of the Normans significantly over the next few years. In 1029, Duke Sergius IV of Naples regained

his throne, largely through the efforts of a certain Rainulf
and his Norman band. In the following year, Sergius built
a castle at Aversa which was given to Rainulf to hold as a
Neapolitan outpost on the border with Capua, and with
the castle went the hand of the duke's sister and a considerable grant of land. This was an event of decisive importance, for it marked the beginning of the end of the Normans as mere mercenaries fighting for whichever employer
would pay them best. At least one of the hired captains
had become a territorial lord in his own right, with a castle
and rich lands. Soon other Lombard princes followed the
example of Sergius, and at least a dozen Normans were
established on the land. Finally, in the spring of 1038,
Rainulf, who had transferred his allegiance from Naples
to Capua, was formally invested as count of Aversa by the
Holy Roman Emperor Conrad II, during one of his Italian
expeditions.

With this event, feudalism may be said to have entered
southern Italy. These Norman feudatories soon became a
law unto themselves and were scarcely distinguishable
from robber barons. The political circumstances—the
struggle between the Lombard duchies and the maritime
cities, the rivalry between the Byzantine and the Holy
Roman empires, the chronic revolts in Apulia—played
directly into Norman hands. It was certainly possible,
should an able leader emerge, that all of southern Italy
would become Norman.

Thus of equal importance with the settlement of Norman soldiers on the land was the appearance in Italy, in
1032, of the first of the sons of Tancred d'Hauteville. After
his acquisition of Aversa, Rainulf had sent letters back to
Normandy inviting his compatriots to come seek their

fortunes in Italy. Among those who responded were William and Drogo d'Hauteville, sons of a minor Norman tenant. They were followed over a period of years by their brothers Humfrey, Serlo, Robert, Tancred, Mauger, a second William, Geoffrey, and Roger. The first William and Drogo at once sold their swords to Pandulf III of Capua, who, with their aid and that of Rainulf of Aversa, took Gaëta, Amalfi, and Sorrento.

From this time on the Normans pursued a policy of relentless self-aggrandizement at the expense of their nominal feudal superiors and of the Byzantines. Although the course of conquest was broken by setbacks and defeats, there was a steady growth of Norman power during the middle decades of the eleventh century. As early as 1040 the Norman mercenaries in Greek service turned against their employers and, joining forces with Apulian malcontents, seized the towns of Melfi and Venosa. A strong castle was built at Melfi, where the Norman commanders, Arduin and Ralf, are said to have mustered 500 knights. In the spring of 1041 a joint Lombard-Norman army took the field. Although the 2000 knights attributed to the Norman contingent is probably too high, the addition of the heavy cavalry to the traditional Lombard infantry formations proved decisive. On 4 May the confederates met the army of the Byzantine catapan, Doceanus, at Monte Maggiore, on the river Ofanto. The Norman knights rode down the elite units of the Varangian Guard, and Doceanus was decisively defeated. The government at Constantinople then posted its best general, George Maniakes, to Italy, but he soon was driven to revolt and returned to the Balkans, where he was eventually assassinated. This left the Normans virtually a free hand. Although they were nominally in the service of Gaimar IV of Salerno, they claimed all Greek territory theirs by right of conquest. The prince of Salerno was given the title of duke of Apulia, but beyond the right of exacting military service and of recognizing by deed or charter the lands expropriated by the Normans, the title meant very little. Gaimar's outwardly imposing political position in essence rested on the lances of his Norman vassals, and it might be overturned at any time.

Among themselves, the Normans divided Apulia into twelve counties; twelve of the leaders were chosen as counts. Melfi was selected as the capital of Norman Apulia, and in February 1043, William d'Hauteville was elected count of Apulia, thus acquiring a vague superiority over the other counts. When Count William died toward the end of 1045, his brother Drogo was recognized as his successor. Too late, Apulian rebels and Lombard dukes realized what was happening in southern Italy. Town after town, from Monte Gargano to the river Crati, fell before the inexorable pressure of the Normans.

Their siege tactics were simple but effective; all the entrances to a town were blockaded, and the population was starved into surrender, for the Byzantine catapan could spare no troops for relief operations. A captured town was secured by a temporary ring-work or motte-and-bailey castle until more permanent fortifications could be erected. After a town or valley was thus occupied, a stone castle soon rose on some neighboring spur of the Apennines to dominate the conquered territory. The Normans also pursued a policy of deliberate and ruthless terror against the civilian population, which soon learned that the new masters were a far greater scourge than the old.

In 1047, the position of the Normans in southern Italy was legalized when Emperor Henry III, during an expedition into Italy, recognized Rainulf of Aversa and Drogo of Apulia as imperial vassals. Before this, the Hauteville brothers had been merely the elected commanders of the Norman military companies—little more than "chairmen of the board." But with his imperial investiture as count of Apulia, Drogo acquired sovereignty, in theory at least. Whether, and to what extent, it could be exercised over the turbulent Norman barons remained to be seen. To old Italian hands, submission to the lately arrived Hautevilles seemed almost degrading, and a strong hand was always required to produce even a semblance of order in Apulia.

The turning point came in 1057. Count Drogo had been murdered in 1051 by Lombard conspirators, and was succeeded in turn by his brother Humfrey, who died in 1057. The Norman magnates thereupon elected a fourth brother, Robert Guiscard, as count. He was, perhaps, the only man who could impose order on the unruly tenants of Apulia. Although Guiscard was troubled with feudal disorder at home and with intervention by the papacy, the Holy Roman emperor, and the Byzantine emperor, he proceeded methodically to subjugate most of southern Italy. In 1060 the last Byzantine outpost in Calabria was taken; in the same year, in cooperation with his brother Roger, he began the conquest of Sicily, although it required thirty years to complete. After a long siege, Bari, the last Byzantine foothold in Italy, surrendered in 1071, and in 1073, Amalfi was compelled to acknowledge Guiscard's overlordship. Finally, in 1076, the Lombard duchy of Salerno fell into his hands. Only Benevento, Capua, and Naples remained independent of the duke of Apulia, as Robert was now styled. Naples maintained a precarious independence for another sixty years; Capua had been seized in 1058 by Richard of Aversa, nephew and successor of the first count, Rainulf. There now existed two major Norman states in Italy, destined to become bitter rivals for the better part of a century.

Not a great deal is known about the feudal institutions of Norman Italy. Much of Apulia had been conquered on a sort of free-lance basis, and the lords of such territories were inclined to regard themselves as "the men of no man": that is to say, they held their lands of no feudal superior. Although it is recorded that military service was rigorously exacted by Guiscard, the regularity with which his tenants revolted is some indication of the difficulties he faced. The seige of Benevento in 1077 had to be lifted so that the duke could deal with a baronial rising; for a like reason, in 1083, Guiscard had to abandon a hitherto successful campaign against the Byzantine empire in Epirus.

Baronial risings were certainly not unknown in Capetian France, Norman England, and elsewhere in feudal Europe, but nowhere were they as widespread or as difficult to suppress as in Apulia. One obvious reason was the difficulty of the terrain. Norman tenants, planted in the innumerable mountain valleys of western Apulia and the lower Abruzzi, could only with difficulty and patience be forced into loyalty to the duke. The campaigns of Guiscard and his successors against rebellious vassals included few pitched battles. Instead, they consisted of continuous sieges of mountain castles and isolated little towns. And in a few years, the castles and towns had to be besieged again.

A complicating factor was that, to a degree unknown elsewhere, powers hostile to the establishment of a strong state in southern Italy were able to use the chronic discontent of the Norman tenants to further their own ambitions. Thus the papacy emerged as the champion of feudal and civic liberties. Both the Holy Roman and Byzantine emperors had political and territorial claims to prosecute. A rebellion fomented by the Byzantine Emperor Alexius I brought Duke Robert back to Italy in 1083.

Not much information is available about the composition of the armed forces of southern Italy and Sicily before the middle of the twelfth century. In contrast to the mainland, Sicily was singularly free from feudal strife. The conquest of the island was principally the work of the youngest of the Hauteville brothers, Roger, although on occasion he had some assistance from Robert Guiscard. Count Roger's subordinates—Norman, French, and Italian adventurers—were always kept under firm control, and always knew who was in charge. In the early phases of the conquest, during the 1060's, it seems unlikely that the forces at Roger's disposal amounted to more than 600 knights; in fact, for the operations of 1062, he had only 130 heavy cavalry at his command. Two enfeoffments (the granting of land in return for military service) are known to have been made: one in 1072, after the capture of Palermo, and another in 1091, after the occupation of the island was complete. It is significant that no single fief was of any great extent, and the count was careful not to grant any dangerous immunities to his tenants.

The amount of knight service due from the Sicilian vassals is, however, unknown. About the mainland more information is available, although it must be used with caution. For the reign of King Roger (1105–1154) a survey has survived, the *Catalogus Baronum,* which antedates by some years the similar English *Cartae Baronum* of 1166. It is, of course, very risky to argue that a mid-twelfth-century document reflects conditions of a generation or two earlier. Service was, however, based on the fundamental Norman institution of the knight's fee, with groupings of five and ten knights, reminiscent of the controversial constabulary of Norman England. Other evidence shows a forty-day annual period of service, although some tenants seem to have been obligated for sixty days. To insure the proper performance of a tenant's military duty, the Assize of Ariano (1140) stipulated that among treasonable practices punishable by death or confiscation were desertion in battle, the surrender of castles, the arming of mobs, and the refusal to aid the king's troops or those of his allies. The number of knights due from mainland vassals can be only partially estimated, for while the *Catalogus* covers most of Norman Italy, Calabria is omitted altogether. In this limited territory there were 3,453 knightly tenants, more or less. Some of these held directly of the crown; others were undertenants.

In one important respect the *Catalogus* does not reflect conditions in the eleventh century. Following the great rebellions of 1132–1134 and 1135–1139, the lands of King Roger's most dangerous enemies were confiscated, and their holders were exiled. This sweeping dispossession, which has no parallel elsewhere, was possible largely because of the nonfeudal resources of the crown, which made it less dependent on feudal service than was Norman England or Capetian France. To reduce further the opportunities for baronial disturbances, either public or private, royal permission was required to build castles, as in Normandy and Norman England.

Royal monopolies on forests, mines, and quarries had military implications. The products were necessary in the manufacture of arms and the construction of castles. Because the natural resources were under strict royal control, private individuals had a difficult time procuring the means with which to defy the crown.

Military service was a duty imposed upon the entire population. It has been estimated that about half of the armed forces of the combined kingdom of lower Italy and Sicily were furnished by the tenants-in-chief and their knights, by the towns, and by the rural population. Besides the knightly class, freeholders of the lesser sort, comparable to the sergeants of France and England, are mentioned, and even serfs and villeins could be summoned to arms by means of the *arrière-ban* (the summons calling out the whole mass of subjects). In addition to the customary annual service of forty days, tenants were obligated to provide castle-guard and coast-watch. Holders of some fiefs were additionally required to help furnish and equip galleys for naval service. This obligation, however, fell most heavily upon the coastal towns, particularly those in Sicily, for the mainland ports had been quite successful in securing either total exemption or a considerable reduction in the naval service due.

But the backbone of the army, from the days of Count Roger in the eleventh century to those of Manfred in the thirteenth, consisted of Moslem mercenaries. As they did in England, the Normans took over those native institutions which were more advanced than their own; the influence of Moslem administrative machinery is clearly seen in the operations of the government of Sicily. It was the function of the Treasury to provide funds for military and naval purposes, and its efficiency made it possible for the counts—later, kings—to maintain what amounted to a permanent army and navy. The standing army was predominately Moslem. The mercenaries seem to have been enlisted by officers of their own faith (*kaids*) who were drawn from the native aristocracy (*Djunds*). On campaign they were employed primarily as infantry and as horsed archers. These troops were especially trusted by Norman rulers, as they were immune to papal tampering. Since they owed their personal safety to the prosperity of the count or king alone, they were above suspicion. The Moslems were also highly respected as military engineers. At the siege of Montepelosa (1133), Moslems worked the movable towers, and half a century later, at the siege and taking of Thessalonica, the breach in the wall was made by huge mangonels (stone-throwing machines) constructed by Moslem engineers.

The command structure of the army was simple. Usually the count or king commanded in person, but if military operations were being conducted in widely separated localities, the chancellor, though invariably a cleric, was entrusted with an independent command. Guarin and Robert of Selby, King Roger's chancellors, commanded armies, administered military areas, and were empowered to conduct negotiations of war, peace, and alliance. The chancellorship had a more military character than was usual in western kingdoms. In Norman and early Plantagenet England, for example, these functions were frequently entrusted to the justiciar; in the absence of the king he was, to all intents and purposes, a viceroy. The only other military official of note in the Sicilian kingdom was the constable, who supervised the feudal levies.

The navy was scarcely less important than the army. Robert Guiscard had been well aware of the significance of sea power, and the successful sieges of Bari (1071), Palermo (1072), and Salerno (1076) were due in large part to effective cooperation between land and naval forces. Interest in sea power declined during the reigns of Guiscard's two weak successors in Apulia, but it was revived by Count, later King, Roger. Indeed, the governing of two land areas separated by water as a single state would have been impossible without a navy strong enough to insure uninterrupted communications between them at all times. As is noted above, the provision of ships and men was a condition of tenure in many instances. The coast towns of Sicily and, to a greater or less extent, those of the mainland were, like the English ports obligated to provide ships with full complements for the royal service.

In organizing the navy, it seems probable that the Normans adapted to their own purposes procedures that were already customary in Apulia and Sicily. The Byzantines had regularly requisitioned the larger types of merchant vessels in the ports of Langobardia—ships which were capable of carrying men and horses. It is certain that for the early campaigns in Apulia and Sicily, the Normans relied on available local shipping for amphibious operations; only in 1076 is there specific mention of Norman shipbuilding activities, in connection with an expedition against Trapani. A navy department existed, with a count of the galleys who was charged with supervising the tenants and towns that owed naval service.

If the naval procurement service was derived from Byzantine practice, the sea command derived exclusively from Moslem precedent. The Arab sea-"emir" became the Latin "ammiratus," which, in time, was transmuted into "admiral." It is interesting to note that the first and greatest of King Roger's admirals were Greek. Christodulus held the high naval command from 1110 to 1130, and he was followed by George of Antioch, who commanded until about 1150. The latter was a man of exceptional ability. The powerful fleets under the command of these sea dogs made it possible for King Roger to pursue an aggressive foreign policy and to establish a short-lived protectorate over the coast of North Africa from Tunis to Tripoli.

Land warfare in Norman Italy presents few points of interest. One of these is the continual military intervention in lower Italy of papal and imperial armies. Both popes and Holy Roman emperors had territorial and jurisdictional claims in the south, and neither wished to see a powerful state established there. As often as not, papal or imperial expeditions resulted in meaningless treaties and submissions, but occasionally serious fighting took place. Such fighting occurred in the campaign of 1053. At this time the Norman hold on southern Italy was far from secure. The Byzantines were still in possession of key points in Apulia; much Norman-occupied territory was in open revolt. To Pope Leo IX (1049–1054) the circumstances seemed propitious for getting rid of the troublesome Normans. An agreement was reached with the Byzantine catapan, Argyrus, for action against the scattered Norman bands. A papal army, marching by way of Monte Cassino and Benevento, was to join the Byzantine forces at Siponto, on the Adriatic coast. Thence the confederates in overwhelming strength would march to crush the Normans. The army assembled by the pope was a motley host. It included Lombard contingents from Fermo, Spoleto, Teano, Aquino, and Benevento, as well as troops supplied by such lesser dynasts as the duke of Gaëta. The steadiest component of Pope Leo's army was a body of 700 Swabian mercenary infantry brought to aid the papal cause by Cardinal Frederick of Lorraine and commanded by counts Werner and Adalbert.

Faced by a common threat, the Normans for the moment put aside their differences and united to prevent a junction of the papal and Byzantine forces. An army, allegedly of 3000 knights, was mustered in which the principal commanders were Richard of Aversa and the Hauteville brothers, Humfrey and Robert Guiscard of Apulia. There is no mention of additional troops, so it must be supposed that these knights constituted the entire Norman army. Thrusting themselves between the advancing papal army and the Byzantines at Siponto, the Normans confronted the enemy near Civitate (Civitella), in the valley of the river Fortore. It was a precarious position, certainly, but under the circumstances the risk seemed justifiable. When parleys with the pope broke down, the Norman commanders, although their forces were outnumbered, decided to bring on a general action. The army was deployed in three divisions, apparently two in line and one in reserve. Richard of Aversa commanded the right wing, Humfrey of Apulia the left, with Robert Guiscard in charge of the reserve.

Although the papal army is said to have been larger, no figure is given as to its actual size. It probably contained some mounted troops. If the chronicler is correct in his statements, the pope's command consisted of 700

German infantry and the Italo-Lombard units, which numbered in excess of 2,300. The entire papal force seems to have been deployed in line, with the Swabians on the right and the Italo-Lombards holding the remainder of the front.

The battle of Civitate (17 June 1053) was opened by the Normans, who launched an attack along the entire line. The division commanded by Richard of Aversa made short work of the levies from the Italian towns, who soon broke and were driven from the field. But Humfrey of Apulia could make no headway at all against the German infantry. Even when the reserve under Guiscard was committed, the Swabians stubbornly held their ground. Victory was assured only when Richard of Aversa returned from his pursuit of the papal left and joined in the assault. The Germans, to the last man, died where they stood.

The victory at Civitate was decisive in the history of the Norman conquest, for in essence it gave lower Italy to the Hautevilles; the Greeks were in no position to continue the contest alone. It is, moreover, of interest for its military implications. If the chronicler of the battle, William of Apulia, is at all accurate, it would appear that 700 mercenary infantry could fight 2,000 knights to a standstill, and that only the intervention of an additional 1,000 assured victory to the Normans. It would be helpful, of course, to know something about the terrain on which the Swabians were posted; it would also be useful if the figure of 3000 knights could be verified. It would then be easier to assess the military significance of the action. However, in spite of the ambiguities, it seems quite clear that in the middle of the eleventh century good infantry—in this instance, professional—if the odds were at all favorable, could hold their position against what was generally regarded as the best feudal horse of the day. This was to be proven again at Hastings thirteen years later.

The battle of Nocera (24 July 1132) also is of interest, by reason of the tactical formations adopted by the opposing commanders. The campaign of 1132, of which this action was an incident, stemmed from a revolt which broke out against King Roger on the mainland in September 1131. Capua, Naples, Amalfi, the Lombard towns, and the Norman barons of Apulia were resolved to shake off their allegiance to Roger, who had assumed the royal title in 1130. Early in 1132, Amalfi and Naples were restored to royal control, but Robert II of Capua and Rainulf of Avellino, an Apulian baron of considerable military ability, were still in the field with large forces. Robert is alleged to have mustered an army of 3000 knights and 40,000 foot—numbers which are certainly inflated. No figures are given for the size of the army under King Roger's command. In the late spring or early summer of 1132, the two armies were hovering in the vicinity of Benevento, each hoping to gain the active support of its citizens. But the Beneventans wisely declared themselves neutral, and King Roger, who was not in sufficient force to risk a general action so far from his base of operations, began a withdrawal in the direction of Salerno. He was followed so closely by Duke Robert that the withdrawal became a precipitate retreat in which the Moslem infantry of the king's rear guard suffered heavily. Roger, however, managed to get his army safely across the river Sarno near its junction with the Sabato and to destroy the bridge behind him. So that the campaign would not seem to be a total loss, he then laid siege to the nearby castle of Nocera.

Duke Robert, with the aid of Rainulf of Avellino, constructed a new bridge and forced the crossing of the Sarno in the face of heavy resistance. At once the rebels drew up a line of battle on the level ground between the river and Nocera—a dangerous tactical position, for with the river at their backs, there would be scant possibility of an orderly retreat across the single bridge over the Sarno. This was similar to the position held by the Lancastrian army at Tewkesbury in 1471, during the English Wars of the Roses, with a single bridge across the Avon at its back. The order of battle adopted by Robert and Rainulf was somewhat unusual. Their combined forces were divided into two wings, or corps, with Robert commanding the right and Rainulf the left. Each commander, in turn, organized his available troops into three divisions; in view of the rather complicated order, it must be suspected that plans had been made before the crossing of the Sarno. Duke Robert massed his three divisions in column. His first division consisted of mounted troops, the second was composed of his infantry units to support the cavalry, and the third division was also mounted, either to act as a reserve or to be held in readiness for a pursuit. Count Rainulf, whose command seems to have consisted entirely of cavalry, deployed his three divisions in line, with 250 knights detached to make contact with the garrison in Nocera. Moreover, the count refused the flank divisions which served to protect the left flank of the army.

The king had no choice but to accept the challenge of battle. He drew up his army in column, eight divisions deep, opposite Duke Robert's wing of the rebel army. This, as has been noted earlier, was a fairly common medieval order of battle, although it was never very successful, and the French were still using it as late as the early fifteenth century, with disastrous results. Neither the number nor the proportion of cavalry to infantry in the royal army is stated.

The initiative was taken by King Roger, who launched his leading division, swords drawn, against the opposing line. The impetus of the charge drove the Capuan knights back on their infantry support, which broke and made for the flanks and rear. The single span across the Sarno was choked with fugitives, a thousand of whom are alleged to have drowned. The majority, however, escaped by fleeing over the level ground to the right and left rear.

The third division of Duke Robert's corps, which had opened ranks to let the infantry and the wrecks of the first division through, now reformed and charged in upon the disordered first royal division and the second, which had by this time also been committed. The Capuans were, however, unable to make any headway against the royalists; indeed they were beginning to give ground. Then came the decisive moment. Count Rainulf, whose corps seems to have been unengaged until this point, wheeled to the right, and with the center division of five hundred knights leading, charged into the right flank of King Roger's leading elements. His right and left divisions provided successive shocks as they came into action. Heartened by the timely aid, the Capuan cavalry rallied and returned to the charge.

The flank attack, in addition to the stiffening resistance along the line, was too much for King Roger's two committed divisions; they broke, and in their flight they carried away the remaining divisions of the royal army. In vain the king attempted to rally his fleeing knights; then, realizing that the day was irretrievably lost, he turned from the stricken field, accompanied, according to the chronicler, by only four knights, and joined his troops in flight. With Count Rainulf in hot pursuit, the king and his slender escort galloped into Salerno at sundown, and the gates were slammed shut, literally in the face of the enemy. The disaster was complete. King Roger's camp fell into the hands of the victors; more than seven hundred knights were taken prisoner, and the infantry of the royal army was cut to pieces in the pursuit. Moreover, the rebel victory intensified the revolt throughout mainland Italy.

But when the aid promised to the rebels by the Holy Roman emperor failed to materialize, the king eventually was able to crush the insurgents. That Sicily remained loyal, providing Roger with resources in men and money, was a crucial factor in these later developments. Count Rainulf was able to inflict another defeat on the king at Rignano (30 October 1137), under conditions similar to those at Nocera, but the death of the count of Avellino in April 1139 removed the one rebel commander of real military ability. By the end of the year Roger's writ again ran throughout the mainland territories.

Of much greater interest than the land actions in Norman Italy is the development of a very effective combination of military and naval forces that made possible the conquest of Sicily and of a considerable stretch of the North African coastline. The cooperation by land and sea was also invaluable in the reduction of coastal towns where neither arm alone would have been successful. Even before the mainland conquests were secure, the assault on Sicily had begun. The capture of Reggio di Calabria by Guiscard in 1060 provided the necessary base, and almost at once preparations were started for an invasion of the island. The conquest of Sicily was no doubt facilitated by the inability of the three Moslem emirs who divided the island to combine against the Normans, but the military factor of chief significance was the ability of the invaders to put troops ashore at the time and place of their own choosing. In 1060 a party of 60 knights was landed near Messina. When a detachment of the city garrison issued out, the Normans, by means of a feigned flight, drew the Moslems to a safe distance beyond the walls, then turned on their pursuers and drove them back into Messina. The second landing, in the spring of 1061, might be termed a reconnaissance in force. Some 160 knights were put ashore without opposition and spent several days on the island— partly because rough seas which prevented their re-embarkation—before recrossing the Straits of Messina. The information gathered from these two brief forays seems to have convinced Guiscard and his brother Roger that Messina was vulnerable and that a permanent lodgment on the island could be effected. So after a naval reconnaissance, thirteen ships landed 270 knights and their horses by night at Tremestrieri, some four and a half miles south of Messina. The landing seems to have been completely unexpected and unobserved, for it is related that the first wave slept for the remainder of the night and did not put on its fighting gear until morning. At this time, a high Moslem official (*kaid*) with an escort of 30 troops was encountered. The escort was routed, and the *kaid* and a large sum of money were captured. Later in the morning the ships, which had shuttled back to Reggio, returned with an additional 170 knights and their mounts, bringing the total strength to 440. As this small army approached the city, the garrison fled by land and by sea, and Messina was occupied without resistance. Meanwhile, the transports continued to shuttle back and forth between Sicily and the mainland until the number of mounted troops had been built up to 1,000 and a like number of infantry had been landed.

The conquest of Messina gave the Normans a secure bridgehead and a base for future operations in the island. It also gave them command of the Straits of Messina, which had considerable commercial and military significance. The ships used to ferry troops across the strait do not seem to have been designed primarily as military transports; the carrying capacity was not large—approximately twenty knights and their mounts. In all probability the Normans acquired the technical knowledge from the Byzantines or from sailors in Byzantine Italy. In 1038, Norman mercenaries formed part of a Byzantine army that landed in Sicily in an unsuccessful attempt to reconquer it from the Moslems. Ships from Reggio took part in the first Sicilian expeditions, and on later campaigns sailors and vessels from Apulian and Calabrian ports are mentioned. The Byzantine fleet was, of course, accustomed to transporting horses, and special ships had been designed for this purpose, but there is no indication that any such vessels were stationed in Italian waters. In all probability, the ships used by the Normans in the eleventh century were large trading galleys fitted with some sort of temporary boxes to prevent damage to the valuable and fragile horses. It would be rash to argue that the Norman Normans did not know how to transport horses by water, but it is noteworthy that Apulians, Calabrians, and Sicilians served in the army that fought under Duke William at

Hastings.[1] Perhaps these adventurers were able to give the duke some assistance in solving his transportation problems.

The Normans were also quick to utilize sea power in the reduction of the coastal towns of lower Italy and Sicily. The most dramatic of the combined operations was the siege of Bari, which began in 1068 and ended with the capitulation of the last Byzantine stronghold in Italy on 16 April 1071. The city was completely surrounded by land and by sea, with the ships nearest the shore being connected to it by bridges. Although some ships managed to slip through the cordon to summon aid, and although some grain was brought in by blockade-runners, the defeat of a large relieving fleet early in 1071 persuaded the garrison that further resistance was hopeless. In this engagement nine of twenty Byzantine warships were sunk.

As soon as Bari had been captured and its shipping facilities were available, Guiscard and Count Roger turned their attention to the great Sicilian port of Palermo. The campaign was well planned and soundly executed. A fleet of fifty to sixty ships—in contrast to the thirteen for the Messina operation—was collected from Bari and the Apulian towns. Sailing into the vast harbor of Palermo, it put Guiscard and his troops ashore on the east side of the city where the river Oreto flows into the sea. Roger approached from the land side and completed the investment of the town. The Norman blockade failed to close the port completely, and a relieving fleet from Africa was able to break through the naval cordon, but no really

[1] *Widonis Carmen de Hastingae Proelio,* in *Scriptores Rerum Gestarum Willelmi Conquestoris,* ed. J. A. Giles (reprint of 1845 ed.; New York, 1967), p. 34.

effective aid could get into Palermo by sea. To prevent the Moslems of the interior from attempting to raise the siege, Guiscard's nephew Serlo conducted harassing operations in the hills around the Moslem stronghold of Castrogio-vanni. Thus when the final assault was made after a siege of some four months, the defenders of Palermo were so weakened by malnutrition that they were unable to offer effective resistance.

In several respects the Norman conquest of lower Italy and Sicily is a more impressive achievement than the more celebrated conquest of England by Duke William half a century after the first Normans appeared in Italy. William was ruler of one of the best-run feudal states in Europe, and his resources in men and money were very great. He also had the blessing and moral support of the church behind his enterprise. The Norman adventurers who took service as the hired soldiery of the contending petty princes of southern Italy had nothing but their swords and their native intelligence. The brothers Hauteville seem to have possessed a more than average amount of the latter, and it enabled them within the short space of two generations, despite the opposition of popes and emperors, to build what was perhaps the most powerful of the feudal states of Europe.

But although the *Regno* established by King Roger had a feudal façade, he and his predecessors, with the eclecticism that characterized Norman enterprise everywhere, utilized whatever indigenous institutions they found useful or effective. Nowhere is this more evident than in the sphere of military activities. A continuation of Norman feudal practice established a knightly class upon the land which made available to the dukes of Apulia and the counts of Sicily several thousand heavy-armed cavalry. But the town levies on the mainland continued to be called out, and after the conquest of Sicily, Moslem mercenaries were recruited in large numbers—to the great scandal of the rest of Christendom. Byzantine naval techniques were adopted, and the seaports were compelled to provide men and ships for an effective fleet; after 1076 ships were constructed specifically for combat purposes. It should be noted well that not all these sources of military strength were feudal according to any definition of the term. But drawing on whatever sources of manpower were avaliable, Guiscard and the two Rogers were able to eliminate Lombard and Byzantine rule in lower Italy, to subjugate Moslem Sicily, to frustrate the aggressive designs of popes and Holy Roman and Byzantine emperors, to threaten the very heart of the Byzantine empire on two occasions, and to establish Norman control of the coast of North Africa from Tripoli to Tunis. With the exception of Guiscard and his son Bohemund, whose military activities are noted in a later chapter, no member of the Hauteville family was a particularly good general. But their ability for organization, the magnitude of their resources in men and money, and their knack for selecting able subordinates more than made up for lack of military ability. The Norman state in Italy and Sicily was a truly remarkable creation.

4

The Norman Occupation
of England

That English military institutions in the eleventh century differed notably from those elsewhere is no longer seriously questioned. The contrast with the feudal structure of the contemporary Capetian realm is striking, and English kings had at their disposal a military machine more effective than any west of the Byzantine empire. In England, the obligation of every able-bodied man to serve in the armed forces was no mere theoretical survival from antiquity or souvenir from the Germanic past. In time of invasion, this obligation could be enforced under pain of severe penalty. It seems unlikely that after the first part of the eleventh century this levy, known as the fyrd, was summoned on a large scale, but it survived even the Conquest and was summoned several times thereafter to deal with local emergencies.

The ordinary military needs of kings and subordinate commanders were met by a more specialized type of service, designated by C. W. Hollister as the "select fyrd." [1] For recruiting purposes, the country was divided

1 C. Warren Hollister, *Anglo-Saxon Military Institutions on the Eve of the Norman Conquest* (Oxford, 1962), pp. 38–58.

Map 3. England *ca.* 1070

into units of five hides each—a somewhat arbitrary assessment, since the hidation for military purposes did not always match the actual number of hides on a given estate.[2] Each five-hide unit was required to produce a foot soldier on summons and to provide his pay for as long as sixty days per year. Towns were assessed at an arbitrary number of soldiers. Coastal towns and communities were held responsible for "ship-fyrd"—finding crews and ships for naval service. There is an apparent similarity between this system and the Carolingian grouping of four *mansi* to provide a man for military service. But it has been noted that in the Carolingian empire the practice eventually became a factor in the development of feudalism, because the Franks took to fighting on horseback while the English did not.

Two other sources of military manpower were also available to the English kings. The thegns made up the personal entourage of the kings of the early monarchies as well as of the later kings of the English, the eorls, and other great landed magnates. Often they were given grants of land, but frequently they were landless and were maintained in the households of their patrons. Thegns were under obligation to serve in the royal fyrd. The significant point is that the thegn's military obligation derived from his position in society. He owed military service because he was a thegn, not because he held an estate which carried with it some kind of military obligation. A man who rose from lesser rank to thegnhood assumed this duty, whether or not he held a rood of land.

Another source of military strength in the Old English

[2] The English *hida*, like the Frankish *mansus*, was a unit of land measurement, but its size varied widely from one locality to another.

state consisted of professional mercenary warriors known as *huscarles*. They first appeared in England early in the eleventh century, and were probably instituted by King Cnut (1016–1035). Later, in the reign of Edward the Confessor (1042–1066), *huscarles* were to be found in the military retinues of some of the great eorls. They formed perhaps the strongest element in the royal army during the decade immediately before the Norman invasion. The Old English army was an infantry force, and while there is evidence that on occasion some elements rode to battle, there is no contemporary testimony to indicate that they fought on horseback. The lack of cavalry capability and the obligatory sixty-day period of service were to modify the character of warfare in England after 1066.

Such were the military institutions of the kingdom of the English at the death of Edward the Confessor, when Duke William of Normandy decided to prosecute his rather shadowy claim to the throne by force. The resources of Normandy were, quite obviously, inadequate for so ambitious an undertaking, and William had to augment his army by securing men elsewhere. Mercenaries, both horse and foot, were hired in large numbers. Volunteers, hoping to share in the expected booty, were taken into the duke's employ. All told, it is likely that some six to seven thousand men were recruited. In the strictest sense, it was not a feudal army at all. The duke's Norman tenants must have contributed less than half the total force, and even from the scanty evidence it is fairly certain that many tenants-in-chief did not participate personally in the expedition. A large portion of the force consisted of infantry —spearmen and archers; indeed, the foot soldiers may

have been twice as numerous as the cavalry, if the estimate of two thousand knights is approximately correct.

The duke's plans were bold in conception and daring
in execution. Never since the days of the Roman Empire
had an amphibious operation on such a scale been attempted in western Europe. The assembling of shipping
and transport of men, horses, and supplies in great quantities speak well of the organizing ability of William and
his lieutenants. Medieval armies were notoriously hard
to keep together when there was no fighting in progress,
and while it is not known just when William began to
muster his invasion army, several months elapsed before
it made the Channel crossing in late September.

Hastings has been refought so frequently and in such
detail by so many eminent historians that it is unnecessary
to do more than outline briefly the action and the events
which led up to it. When the favorable wind of 27 September enabled Duke William to launch his cross-Channel
attack, King Harold II of England was in York. Two days
previously he had defeated and killed another claimant to
his throne—King Harald Hardrada of Norway—at the
battle of Stamford Bridge. Thus the Norman army was
able to disembark at Pevensey on the morning of the
twenty-eighth without opposition—a great stroke of luck.
Although Harold marched from York as soon as he got
word of the Norman landing, it is doubtful that he could
have reached London before 9 October, and then only
with such troops as were mounted; thus William had
time to consolidate a bridgehead on the Hastings peninsula. Marching from London, probably on the tenth, with
his tired *huscarles* and such local shire levies as could be

hastily mobilized, the king failed to surprise the Normans in their camp. On the night of the thirteenth, the English went into bivouac at Senlac, seven miles north of Hastings. Their approach had been reported to William during the afternoon, and shortly after sunrise on the fourteenth, the Norman army marched to meet the enemy in three divisions, brigaded as it was to fight. As the invaders deployed some two hundred yards in front of the English position, each division consisted of three lines—archers, spearmen, and cavalry—from front to rear. Apparently the archers and infantry were to effect breaches in the enemy line that could be exploited by the knights. This was, for the eleventh century, an ingenious and complicated battle plan, but no provision was made for a tactical reserve. The English army was deployed on the Senlac ridge, just below the crest, in a single line, with the most reliable troops, the *huscarles*, in the front ranks.

The action began at about nine o'clock, and from the beginning, nothing seemed to go right with the duke's plan. Not only did the archers and spearmen fail to make any impression on the English line; a counterattack carried away the Breton infantry and its cavalry support on William's left. Only by detaching from the uncommitted Norman cavalry of the center was the counterstroke repulsed, with heavy losses to the English. The duke then launched the knights of the third line against the enemy position, and this time it was the Norman center that gave way and was pursued down the slope by the English. At this point the invading army seemed on the verge of disintegration. This incident gave rise to the celebrated "feigned flight" story, which almost certainly was invented by Norman historians to conceal the fact that the Norman knights were very nearly beaten by the English.[3] While the feigned flight was a tactical device known to European commanders in the eleventh century, it was not a battle-field improvisation. Its successful employment required careful planning and coordination; on no other occasion is it alleged to have been thought of and put into execution on the spur of the moment.

Only by dint of hard fighting was the situation restored. After about six hours of combat, the English still held their position on the ridge, although casualties had caused them to shorten their front. With little more than two hours of daylight remaining, a Norman victory would have to be won quickly. While the archers directed a plunging fire into the English ranks, the duke ordered a general attack all along the line— by spearmen, unhorsed knights, and those who still retained their horses. On the Norman left, where the slope was easier, the attackers succeeded in taking the English line in flank and rolling it up. A band of Norman knights cut its way through to the king's command post. There Harold was slain, on the spot where the high altar of Battle Abbey was later to stand. As darkness fell, the remnants of the English army withdrew into the forest, with the *huscarles* resisting stubbornly to the end, even administering a sharp check to a detachment of knights that pursued too closely.

William now faced the problem of how to exploit his victory. King Harold and his two able brothers, Gyrth and

[3] Norman chroniclers asserted that Duke William, after his original battle plans failed to produce results, ordered a deliberate "flight" to draw the English out of their lines. The ruse is alleged to have been successful, but many modern authorities have serious doubts, as is indicated above.

Leofwine, had perished in the battle, but William certainly knew that their deaths did not mean the collapse of all resistance. Only a small fraction of the military resources of the kingdom had been present on the field of Hastings, and it was possible that the English would rally under other leaders. So William returned to his base at Hastings, where he remained for five days reorganizing his army. Deciding to secure his communications with Normandy instead of striking directly for London or Winchester, he marched eastward along the coast, seizing the ports, in case he should find it necessary to retreat. Folkstone and King Harold's new castle at Dover were occupied without resistance. After a halt due to an outbreak of dysentery, the march was resumed, and Canterbury submitted. From here the Norman line of march followed the old trackway along the South Downs later known as the Pilgrim's Way, which swings in a wide arc from Canterbury across Kent and Surrey, below London, and on into Berkshire. As the Normans passed London south of the Thames, a strong mounted column made a dash on the metropolis, defeating a force of Londoners at Southwark but making no attempt to force the river crossing and seize the city. After burning Southwark, the column rejoined the main body. The army marched in two, sometimes three columns as it moved westward—not so much because of tactical considerations as because of the sheer necessity of feeding the soldiers who lived off the country through which they moved. Had the army been restricted to a single road, the center and rear elements would have found slim pickings indeed. At about the time the Normans crossed into Berkshire, considerable numbers of reinforcements seem to have joined the army, by way of Chichester. At about this time also, Winchester submitted to the conqueror. Winchester functioned in some ways as a capital for England, so now William was in possession of two of the most important towns in the kingdom—Canterbury and Winchester.

The duke then concentrated his army at Wallingford, on the south bank of the Thames, which he crossed about the middle of November. Again the invaders marched in three columns in a wide sweep, this time to the west and north of London. Bedford was occupied, and a raiding column pushed eastward as far as Cambridge. London was now effectively sealed off from the rest of the country, with William's army astride the two main roads from the north. About the beginning of December, the Norman army began to concentrate in the vicinity of Hertford, and shortly thereafter the English magnates submitted to William at Berkhamstead.

Thus ended a campaign which had lasted, from beginning to end, for some seven or eight months—a campaign without parallel in eleventh-century annals until the First Crusade. That it was not a typically "feudal" campaign is at once apparent. Yet the commander of the expedition was a typical "feudal" prince. Again it becomes obvious that when feudal sources of manpower were inadequate, commanders utilized any others that were within their means.

After a brief period in which King William tried to govern through the existing civil and ecclesiastical hierarchy, the Norman regime became essentially military in character, based upon castles and what amounted to an army of occupation. The estates of the vanquished English in occupied areas were bestowed on reliable laymen and clerics. On these in turn were imposed military quotas which seem to have been purely arbitrary and which bore no relation to the size or value of the fee (estate) involved. These quotas were definitely established by 1070, and they reflect the military necessities of the period 1067–1070 when the permanence of the Norman occupation hung in the balance. It is also certain that by means of these feudal grants King William assured himself of the service of between five and six thousand knights, no matter how the tenants might see fit to raise them. It is futile to speculate about the length of service required of these contingents. For many of them, these years of revolt and invasion must have been years of almost continuous service.

Instrumental in the preservation of the Norman Conquest was the large-scale construction of castles throughout the occupied areas. Castles had appeared in England during the reign of Edward the Confessor, when a few had been constructed by that king's Norman favorites, and at least one such fortress had been erected at Dover by King Harold. The virtue of the motte-and-bailey castle, of course, was its simple plan and the rapidity with which the structure could be thrown up; it is not surprising that such castles appeared, literally by the hundreds, throughout Norman England. They varied greatly in size and complexity. Some were simple mottes; others may have been elaborations of earlier English ring-works. Many were constructed by royal authority; others by great magnates; still others by the lesser tenants of the honorial barons (the undertenants of the great magnates). Singly, each provided a base from which the surrounding district might be dominated or which afforded at least a temporary refuge in case of an uprising or an invasion. Collectively, they formed a network of fortifications which must have discouraged local rebels or foreign invaders. All important towns were provided with castles, even when their construction involved the destruction of urban tenements. Road junctions and river crossings were guarded by castles. Indeed, when the locations of the castles of the Conquest are plotted on a map, it is virtually impossible to find a spot of strategic importance which did not have a castle in the immediate vicinity. Castle-guard was part of a knight's normal military obligation in time of peace as well as of war.

Mercenaries were, however, early found in the garrisons of royal castles. As has been noted, there was never a time when the soldier who fought for pay was not available to feudal princes with the money to pay him. The relative affluence of the king-dukes of England-Normandy enabled them to employ mercenary bands whenever a crisis—such as the Danish invasion scare of 1085—required an implementation of normal feudal quotas. The problem boiled down to this: there were never enough Normans to provide, at the same time, garrisons for the numerous castles of strategic significance and a field army with which to face an invasion in force. Princes who could afford them must also have been influencd by the knowledge that professional soldiers were more efficient and more reliable than those who served part-time. After the country had been pacified, campaigns were infrequent except on the Welsh frontier, and as a customary limit of sixty days was set on the length of time a feudal tenant might be required to serve at his own expense, it was natural that rulers should seek to become less dependent on the feudal levy.

By 1100 at the very latest, the kings of England had made it possible for knights to avoid actual military service by a money payment known as scutage. The amount collected was that which would be sufficient to hire a professional soldier for the length of time the tenant would have been obligated to serve. However, in the reign of Henry II the role of the mercenary, or at least that of the paid soldier, began to overshadow that of the feudal tenant. By the end of the twelfth century stipendiary troops, paid from the receipts of the Exchequer, had assumed the primary responsibility for the defense of the realm.

In addition to the feudal levy the post-Conquest kings of England had another significant source of military manpower, the Old English fyrd. References have been made to the employment of native troops even before the pacification was complete, and until the early part of the twelfth century such notices are fairly frequent. The infantry levy was very useful for the siege warfare characteristic of the period, and the Norman kings utilized such troops in their continental wars as well as in purely local operations. Civic levies are mentioned especially during the troubled reign of Stephen. The London militia participated with distinction in campaigns as far afield as Wallingford and Winchester. Little is known about the numerous class of sergeants who appear first in the Domesday Book and later in the Exchequer records known as the Pipe Rolls. These lesser military tenants seem to have constituted the infantry elements—spearmen, archers, and crossbowmen—after the fyrd fell into disuse, although mounted sergeants are also mentioned.

A good deal, thus, is known about the various sources from which the Norman and early Plantagenet kings re-

cruited their armies. A little is also known about conditions
of service, although not as much as may be wished. It will
be remembered that the annual term of service for the
select fyrd was sixty days, and it appears that somehow
William was successful in imposing a similar obligation on
his Norman tenants. At some time during the second
quarter of the twelfth century, probably during the reign
of Stephen, this was reduced to the more conventional
forty days per year. This service was due only for an actual
campaign; the assertion that the knight performed an
annual tour of duty for training lacks any real evidence to
support it. By the beginning of the thirteenth century,
many sergeanties provided much fewer than forty days of
service.

In contrast to field service, castle-guard was an annual
obligation, and the length of service varied widely. In
some castles, Norwich for example, the knights owing
ward (castle-guard) were compelled to serve three tours
of thirty days each; but at Corfe castle, the abbot of
Cerne's knights owed ward for only thirty days.

In sensitive areas, such as the southeast coast and the
exposed Welsh and Scots frontiers, great estates were
created known as castleries (*castelleriae*). These were in
essence rudimentary military districts whose tenants were
bound to provide the garrisons for the major castle in each
district. Knights who owed ward service sought early to
escape the obligation, which was not so much dangerous
as inconvenient, and castle-guard was commuted at rates
far below those required to hire a substitute. Many castles
must, as a result, have contained only skeleton garrisons in
peacetime, with the obligated knights constituting a reserve which could be called up in time of war.

The problems of maintaining adequate garrisons must also have contributed to the increasing demand for mercenaries. The lord of Harestan castle, in Derbyshire, held a barony of only ten knights' fees, and somehow he had to contrive to garrison his own castle as well as perform ward duty with his knights at Nottingham. Some solution had to be worked out, and mercenaries were the obvious answer.

Before turning to the general characteristics of military operations in the eleventh and twelfth centuries, let us consider briefly what little is known about the organization and command structure of the English armies of that period. The high command was usually the king in person. If he was absent from the country, the command was ordinarily assigned to a close relative or to a high officer of state such as the justiciar. When invasion threatened, regional commands were established, as for example in 1095, when Archbishop Anselm of Canterbury was put in charge of defense measures for southeast England—a most unlikely appointment. There was not, of course, a permanent organization among the contingents making up the royal host. Composition and personnel differed with every campaign; the closest approximation to a military unit was the still shadowy and highly controversial constabulary (*constabularia*), a group of ten knights, which was certainly in existence in the first half of the twelfth century. Since similar groupings of knights are found in Normandy itself and in Norman Italy and Sicily, there seems to be no reason to question its appearance in England. But just how it functioned during actual operations is still unknown.

The infantry levies were usually commanded by the

sheriffs, or other representatives of the crown. It is fairly safe to assume that for any given campaign the available troops were organized and brigaded only when the muster gave the commanding officer an opportunity to see what he was going to have to work with.

During the period between 1066 and the beginning of the thirteenth century, pitched battles were surprisingly few. There was much fighting on the marches of Wales, where warfare was endemic. In England itself, however, the fighting was largely confined to the suppression of baronial revolts until the contest for the throne between King Stephen and the Empress Matilda resulted in operations more nearly approaching the character of formal warfare. In 1075, 1088, 1095, and 1101, the first three Norman kings were faced with revolts by important tenants-in-chief. Henry II was confronted with armed opposition in 1155 and again in 1173–1174. The last rebellion, because it differed in significant ways from earlier ones with similar causes, will be treated separately. The others were basically the same in origin and outcome and can be considered in fairly general terms.

The Anglo-Normans were a turbulent lot. Most of them held lands in the duchy of Normandy as well as in the kingdom of England, and the contrast between the lax rule of Duke Robert and the stern regimes of William II and Henry I was the principal factor in several of these revolts, which usually took a stereotyped course. A group of tenants relying on promised military aid from Normandy would raise the standard of revolt. The king or his lieutenant would move rapidly to isolate the rebels, who would retire to their castles to wait for Norman intervention. The royal forces would then besiege the revolting barons, and when the expected assistance did not materialize, they would be forced to surrender. In this monotonous and far from glamorous siege work, the English fyrd played a significant role. There were, of course, variations on the general theme, but whatever the variations, the end result was the same—and always for the same reason. Even the greatest tenants-in-chief, unlike their contemporaries elsewhere, simply did not have the military resources to defy successfully the power of the crown.

The rebellion of 1173–1174 differed in scope, if not in basic causes. Embracing both England and the Planta-genet possessions in France, it was the most widespread of all the baronial risings. While King Henry II took charge of operations on the Continent, the conduct of affairs in England was entrusted to the justiciar, Richard de Lucy. His basic objective was to keep the centers of rebellion in East Anglia, the Midlands, and Cheshire isolated from each other. To this end royal castles were garrisoned by mercenaries, old motte-and-bailey structures were reconditioned, and at the head of a field army, Lucy began the siege of the rebel stronghold of Leicester in July. He was forced to raise the siege late in the month, when King William of Scotland invaded Cumberland and beseiged Carlisle. The approach of the English army compelled the Scottish king to raise the leaguer and retire across the border, and a truce was concluded, to last until January 1174.

In the meantime, on 29 September, one of the rebel leaders, Earl Robert of Leicester, had landed in Suffolk with a force—doubtfully estimated at three thousand—of French and Flemish mercenaries, most of whom certainly were infantry. This force attempted to thread a cordon of castles held for the king which separated the rebel centers in East Anglia and the Midlands. News of this offensive brought the justiciar south posthaste; Lucy and the constable Humphrey de Bohun, with about three hundred of the king's stipendiary horse, concentrated at St. Edmundsbury. Here they were joined by other royalist troops under earls Reginald of Cornwall, William of Gloucester, and William of Arundel. The royalist army was also augmented by peasants from the surrounding countryside, armed with flails and pitchforks. Altogether Lucy may have disposed of a larger force than did Earl Robert, although its general quality was not as good.

On 17 October 1173, Robert and his mercenaries were marching past St. Edmundsbury in the general direction of Cambridge, without even normal security precautions, although he must have known that the royalist army was in the town. At Fornham, four miles north of St. Edmundsbury, Robert and his men were fording the river Lark when they were attacked by the royal forces. With his army divided by the river, the earl had no chance to deploy to meet the charge. His French mercenary horse were ridden down and captured by the royalists, and the panic-stricken Flemings fled into the marshy meadows of the Lark, where they were hunted down and slain by the peasants. After this victory, hostilities were suspended until after Easter (24 March) 1174.

At the end of March, the Scots, operating in two columns, again crossed the frontier. For the campaign King William had hired a body of Flemish mercenaries. Several castles in Westmorland and Northumberland fell or were besieged early in the campaign. Then the Scots king united his forces and pushed south to the Tyne, where he laid siege to the castle of Prudhoe. An army was hastily mustered at York to relieve the beleaguered castle. King William, upon learning of the advance of a relieving force, lifted the siege of Prudhoe and retreated thirty miles to the north, where he began the siege of Alnwick castle. By early July the Yorkshire army had reached Newcastle-upon-Tyne. On the night of the twelfth, the mounted elements began a forced march which brought them to the vicinity of Alnwick by dawn, where they captured King William as he made an early-morning inspection of his siege lines. To the south the justiciar resumed operations in June when he opened the siege of Huntingdon castle. Early in July the king returned to England and at once took command of the army at Huntingdon. The surrender of the castle virtually marked the end of hostilities.

The details of this revolt reveal the increasing effectiveness of the crown in military matters, due in part to its increasing revenue. For fiscal 1172–1173 direct military expenditures amounted to just over four thousand pounds and for 1173–1174 to more than three thousand pounds—very large percentages of a cash revenue which has been estimated at about twenty-one thousand pounds per annum. With this money castles could be repaired, strengthened, provisioned, and garrisoned. Men whose obligatory service had expired could be continued on active duty. Infantry could be summoned from Shropshire; arrows could be requisitioned in Gloucester, hoes in Worcester; carpenters from Warwickshire and Nottinghamshire could be impressed; and all could be concentrated at Leicester for the prosecution of a siege. By the end of the twelfth century, the king, his castles, and his paid troops were the real core of national defense. The baronial castle, except perhaps on the Welsh Marches, had become obsolete, and the feudal levy, with its unpaid, half-trained contingents was obsolescent, as is strikingly illustrated in the Assize of Arms, issued by Henry II in 1181. Under the provisions of this decree, a free man's military obligations and the type of equipment he must possess no longer depended on his social rank or his landholding status. Henceforth they were determined by the value of his goods and chattels, which might or might not include landed possessions.

In the span of 134 years between 1066 and the end of the twelfth century, there were only three general engagements for which sufficient details survive to permit some comment on their significance or interest. All three occurred during the civil wars of Stephen's reign.

The battle of Northallerton, more commonly referred to as the battle of the Standard, was the climax of another attempt by Scottish kings to profit from disorders within the kingdom to the south. King David I of Scotland had spent the early months of 1138 raiding the northern frontier, secure in the knowledge that King Stephen was fully occupied by a rebellion in the Severn Valley. Toward the end of July the Scots' king launched a formidable offensive which carried, without opposition, all the way to the Yorkshire border. Not until the Scots had reached the Tees was any attempt made to organize resistance. The kings' lieutenant in the north, the aged Archbishop Thurstan of York, then called a council at which it was decided by the principal magnates to muster the military levies of the county.

Nothing is known about the size of the motley host that assembled at York about the middle of August, but its composition can be rather accurately determined. It included the shire levy, with each contingent commanded by its parish priest—perhaps the last historical appearance of the general fyrd. There were, in addition, the *militiae* of York, Beverley, and Ripon, the feudal contingents of the Norman tenants, and some mercenary troops commanded by Bernard de Balliol and Count William of Aumale.

The direction of the campaign seems to have been in the hands of a council of war, with leading roles assigned to Count William and to Walter Espec, sheriff of Yorkshire. By 21 August the army was at Thirsk, about nineteen miles north-northwest of York. Here it was reinforced by contingents from Derbyshire and Nottinghamshire. A reconnaissance revealed that the Scots were across the Tees, twenty-one miles to the north, and were marching south along the Great North Road. A decision to intercept the enemy advance as soon as possible apparently led to a night march, for the Yorkshiremen had covered the eleven miles between Thirsk and the battlefield and had taken up their position before six o'clock on the following morning. The Scots also were on the move early, and the two armies marched toward each other through a dense fog as day began to break.

The Yorkshire army deployed onto high ground to the right of the Great North Road, about three miles north of Northallerton, prepared to meet an attack. Considering the quality of some of the troops, this was doubtless a wise decision. All mounted personnel, with the exception of unit commanders and a small detail to guard the horses, dismounted and fought on foot. The front ranks of a solid phalanx consisted of archers and knights, the latter to prevent the line from being broken by a charge. The remaining knights were posted as a guard around a cart or wagon to which were affixed the standards of St. Peter of York, St. John of Beverley, and St. Wilfrid of Ripon—the only known appearance in England of a practice quite common in the wars among the Lombard cities. The rest of the phalanx was composed of the shire and city levies.

The Scots' order of battle was much more flexible than that of the English, although King David's army also consisted principally of infantry and was equally diversified. The king deployed his forces in five divisions on a hill about four hundred yards from the English position. The center division, composed of the men of Galloway, was somewhat advanced, and the two wings were refused. The right wing, commanded by the king's son, Henry, included a body of knights who retained their horses and seems to have been intended as the main striking force. King David also kept a tactical reserve under his own command, consisting of infantry and a number of dismounted knights.

The action opened at about six o'clock with a charge by the Galwegians, who claimed the honor even though they lacked any sort of armor. Although they suffered heavy casualties, they managed to reach the English line and made a breach in the English front. This was quickly repaired by the dismounted knights, and all subsequent attacks were beaten off. Then Prince Henry launched his wing against the Yorkshire left. His knights covered the distance between the lines in much less time than did their infantry support, and although the Scots cut clear through the English formation, the gap had been closed before the infantry made contact, and the attack was easily repulsed. The Scottish left made but one half-hearted charge, the reserve drifted away, and King David and his knights called for their horses and joined the flight toward their base at Carlisle. By nine o'clock the action was over.

It seems fairly obvious that the Scot's lack of coordination was the prime reason for their loss of the battle. King David had devised an order of battle which potentially could have delivered five successive shocks, but on each occasion the English were allowed time to shore up their line before the next attack was delivered. In all likelihood, the lack of an adequate command structure was responsible for the faulty conduct of the action. Tactical flexibility unsupported by timely execution was not enough to secure victory. As for the English, turning back the invaders was regarded as sufficient. A part of the knightly component was marched away to besiege the castle of a rebellious baron; the rest of the army was disbanded.

While the battle of Lincoln offers little of interest, the operations that preceded it are worth noting. In December of 1140, King Stephen began the siege of Lincoln castle, which had been seized by a clever ruse by Earl Ranulf of Chester. The earl escaped from the castle, returned to Chester about a hundred air miles distant, opened communications with his father-in-law, Earl Robert of Gloucester, in his comital city a hundred miles to the south, mustered his Cheshire tenants, hired Welsh mercenaries, rendezvoused with the Gloucester contingents, and marched about 150 miles in the dead of an unusually wet English winter—all in no more than forty days, a remarkable feat. If the battle that followed had Falstaffian aspects, the organizational capabilities and leadership qualities exhibited by Ranulf and Robert, especially by the former, cannot be faulted.

Their sort of generalship has excited the admiration of historians for centuries, but, because the account of the Lincoln campaign of 1141 has to be pieced together from a variety of sources, it has received less than its just due. By 1 February the two earls were in the vicinity of Lincoln, and King Stephen was finally beginning to believe his intelligence reports. The king was, at the least, a capable general. Possessed of the most limited political insight, he managed to keep the crown on his head for nineteen troubled years only because he was a good fighter. But at Lincoln he was caught off guard, very likely because he could not believe that his enemies would really make an attempt at that time of the year to lift the siege of Lincoln castle. Only when the earls were within a few miles of the city did the king take the elemental precaution of putting a covering force at the crossing of the Fossdyke, a watercourse which lay between the town and the advancing enemy. In the ensuing battle (2 February) the king was defeated and taken prisoner, but the action itself was not unusual.

It has been customary to censure Stephen for his conduct of the battle, and clearly he was outgeneraled by earls Ranulf and Robert. But the historians have wrongly blamed the king. There seems to be no reason to quarrel with his decision to accept a general action outside the walls of Lincoln. He had, according to the best contemporary evidence, the more reliable cavalry and possibly an overall advantage in numbers; he also had the advantage of the ground. His opponents had just completed a long march under adverse conditions, and they must have been pretty wet and cold after fording the Fossdyke on a February morning. Where Stephen was at fault was in his refusal to believe his intelligence reports and to act on them. He had sufficient warning to cause him to strengthen his own forces; even on the day before the battle he might have ensured that the approaches to Lincoln were held in strength enough to prevent an enemy's crossing either the Witham or the Fossdyke. Neither of these precautions was taken, and in the ensuing battle the disgraceful flight of the royalist horse, including the mercenary contingent of the king's ablest lieutenant, William of Ypres—which could not have been anticipated—delivered the king into the hands of his enemies, setting the stage for one of the most interesting campaigns of the entire feudal period.

Following the capture of the king, his rival for the crown, the Empress Matilda, sought to extend her authority over all the kingdom. Resistance, however, was maintained in southeastern England by Stephen's queen—confusingly also named Matilda—and William of Ypres, the king's trusted mercenary captain, who began to redeem his reputation from the shadow cast by his hasty and undignified departure from the field of Lincoln. About the middle of June, the Empress entered London, where her haughty, avaricious conduct soon alienated the Londoners. On 24 June they rose, chased Matilda from the city, and altered the entire political and military situation, as the city was immediately occupied by Stephen's queen.

Bishop Henry of Winchester, who had recognized the Empress, opened negotiations with Queen Matilda and once again became the active supporter of his brother Stephen. He then returned to Winchester, where he laid siege to the royal castle, held by a garrison loyal to the Empress. The Empress was determined to raise the siege of Winchester castle. At her base in Oxford, she mustered an army of her principal supporters. Chief among these was Earl Robert of Gloucester, Empress Matilda's half-brother, the ablest commander among the Angevin partisans. This army must have been of considerable size, including as it did both feudal and mercenary elements. It marched from Oxford, probably on 27/28 July, and appeared under the walls of Winchester on the thirty-first. The Angevin army caught Bishop Henry completely by surprise. He escaped on a fleet horse through one gate of the town as his enemies were marching in, unopposed through another. The bishop's men took refuge in the episcopal castle of Wolvesey, in the southeast corner of the city walls; the Empress set up her headquarters in the royal castle, at the southwest angle of the city; and Earl Robert set up his command post downtown, near the cathedral church of St. Swithun.[4]

Wolvesey castle, a modern fortification erected as recently as 1138, communicated directly with the open field, so its reduction would be a difficult problem for the Angevin assailants. On the second day of hostilities (2 August) the defenders fired the town, probably to deny cover and shelter to the enemy, and a large part of the city was destroyed. Nevertheless, the siege was vigorously pressed. On his escape from Winchester, Bishop Henry hired ad-

---

[4] Winchester was one of the few cities in England with more than one castle. London had three—one a royal castle (the Tower) and two in baronial hands (Baynard's Castle and Montfichet's Castle). There were two royal castles at York and two castles at Winchester, one royal and one episcopal.

ditional mercenaries and exhorted all the kings' supporters
to help raise the siege of Wolvesey castle. The queen,
with a contingent of her own Boulognese tenants, and
William of Ypres, at the head of his Flemish mercenaries,
marched on Winchester immediately. Other important tenants responded to the appeals of the bishop; mercenaries
were also employed in significant numbers, and the London militia, almost a thousand strong, joined the ranks of
the royalists encamped on the eastern side of Winchester.
Here their supply lines were secure, and the chroniclers
note a steady flow of provisions into the camp.

It must have been relatively easy to open communications with the bishop's garrison in Wolvesey castle, but it
is not likely that the royalists were sufficiently numerous to
undertake a regular investment of Winchester. More probably the roads were effectively blockaded and by the beginning of September supplies in the city were running
short, and the pinch of hunger was felt by all within the
walls, civilian and military alike. A desperate attempt to
break the blockade by establishing a fortified post at
Wherwell Abbey, six miles north of the town, was
thwarted, with heavy loss to the Angevins, by William of
Ypres and his Flemings. Earl Robert finally concluded that
the position in Winchester was now untenable and that
there was no alternative to retreat in the face of a superior enemy.

Earl Robert organized the withdrawal carefully. An
elite unit, under the command of Earl Reginald of Cornwall and Brian fitz Count, was given responsibility for the
safety of the Empress and dispatched ahead of the main
body, which guarded the impedimenta. A rear guard under the command of Earl Robert himself was designated

to discourage too vigorous a pursuit. On 14 September, after a fruitless operation of some seven weeks, the Angevin column emerged from the west gate of Winchester and took the Salisbury road, which crossed the river Test at Stockbridge, eight and a half miles to the northwest. But hardly had the retreating army emerged when it was assailed on all sides by the royalists, who swept around the rear guard to fall upon the main body. Unlike the contemporary Syrian Franks, the English had no experience in fighting while on the march, and soon the whole column came apart. The advance guard managed to hold together and eventually reached Gloucester in safety. The main body was destroyed completely; only individual fugitives were able to reach the safety of friendly fortresses. The rear guard fought its way toward Stockbridge, but was forced to a stand, probably because the bridge across the Test was clogged with fugitives. Here it was surrounded by elements of the pursuing army—including the Flemish mercenaries—commanded by Earl William of Surrey and was compelled to surrender. The most important prisoner was Earl Robert of Gloucester, who was eventually exchanged for King Stephen.

The campaign which ended in the Rout of Winchester has been all but neglected by military historians, although it is one of the most fully documented. It was more protracted than usual, and the decisive role played by such nonfeudal elements as mercenary troops and the London militia ought to have attracted more than cursory notice. The conduct of operations by the royalist commander—the professional skills of William of Ypres can be detected—though not spectacular, was effective. No rash or chivalrous actions were undertaken; it was a campaign of outposts and skirmishes except for the action at Wherwell, which involved but a few hundred knights. But slowly the noose tightened around the Empress' army, until, faced with starvation, all they could do was make a run for it. The capture of Earl Robert, the ablest and most respected leader on the Angevin side, nullified all the advantages that faction had gained at the battle of Lincoln seven months earlier.

While pitched battles were somewhat rare, military operations of other types were frequent. The authority of the post-Conquest kings, with the exception of Stephen, saved England from the petty private wars which were prevalent in much of feudal Europe, but on the Scotch and particularly on the Welsh marches warfare was endemic. Before the pacification of England was complete, the first of the Norman marcher lords had begun to encroach upon the lands of their Welsh neighbors, but the rugged character of the terrain, the climate and the primitive character of Welsh society made conquest by ordinary military methods all but impossible. The guerrilla tactics of the Welsh were extremely effective, and not until the late thirteenth century could Wales be considered even reasonably pacified. In this connection one of the very few serious discussions of military matters to appear in feudal Europe was written. In *Descriptio Kambriae* (*ca.* 1194) Gerald of Wales, himself half Welsh and a cleric by profession, outlined the policy of conquest and occupation which was to be carried out successfully by Edward I (1272–1307).

On a smaller scale these methods were pursued by the marcher lords who, for over a century, nibbled away at the lands of the independent Welsh. The key to this expansion was the castle; a broad band of heavily castellated territory extended all the way from the Mersey estuary to that of the Severn. The procedure was simple; as the Normans pushed westward, each new conquest was sealed by the erection of a castle which served as both security and administrative headquarters. The fortifications, usually simple motte-and-bailey structures, could not withstand a determined attack, as their frequent destruction during Welsh risings attests, nor could the Normans permanently occupy the entire country.

By the end of the eleventh century a balance had been struck which was to be maintained with only temporary fluctuations for the next 175 years. At this particular time, the Normans lacked the manpower resources to extend their dominion at the expense of the Welsh, and attempts to do so ended invariably in disaster. On the other hand, the Welsh could seldom forgo their internal feuds in order to unite against the aggressor. Even the opportunity offered by the English civil war of Stephen's reign could not persuade the Welsh princes to cooperate effectively, and although they recovered some territory, the results of their efforts fell far short of what they might have accomplished.

The reign of Stephen, in addition to providing the only pitched battles of the feudal age in England, produced a classic guerrilla campaign and a solution to the problem of irregular warfare which is still useful in the twentieth cenutry. In September 1143, King Stephen, for a variety of very good reasons, arrested Geoffrey de Mandeville, earl of Essex. As soon as he regained his liberty, by surrendering all his castles to the king, the earl retired to the marshes of the Isle of Ely—the fenland area in eastern England which had given even William the Conqueror much trouble—and from this also impregnable strongheld he began to wage a campaign of terror throughout the adjacent portions of Essex, Cambridgeshire, and the Soke of Peterborough. An expedition in the spring of 1144 by King Stephen failed to bring the wily earl to bay. Unable to corner Geoffrey, who exhibited considerable skill as a leader of irregular forces, the king constructed a cordon of castles across the earl's front designed to limit the scope of his depredations. The policy of containment was completely successful. Geoffrey's resources in the fen country were totally inadequate to maintain his forces once they could no longer raid surrounding areas for supplies. By the end of summer, the Isle of Ely and other places under the earl's control literally had been stripped bare, and he had no alternative but to attempt to re-establish communications with his supporters in Essex. This attempt, however, committed Geoffrey to a formal assault on the castle of Burford, held by a royal garrison; in making the assault, he forfeited all the advantages held by a guerrilla force— mobility, elusiveness, and complete freedom of action. As it turned out, Essex was mortally wounded in the unsuccessful attack on Burford and died about a month later. With his death the revolt collapsed, and the king's authority in this part of the kingdom was not challenged for the balance of the reign.

The military history of "feudal" England, from the Conquest to the end of the twelfth century, presents some significant departures from the generally accepted view of medieval warfare. The Norman army that fought the battle of Hastings and engaged in the pacification of England had a liberal infusion of mercenary troops, both infantry and cavalry. The quotas imposed on the tenants-in-chief

(*servitia debita*) cannot be called feudal contracts according to the strict definition of the term, for there seems to
have been no specification as to how these quotas were
to be produced. A tenant could hire mercenaries, maintain
the knights as members of his household, or improvise as
best he could, so long as he fielded the required number
of properly equipped and mounted troops on demand; as
late as 1166, the returns from the *cartae baronum* show
that considerable numbers of knights were still charged to
the demesne—that is, they were maintained in the tenant's
household. As early as 1102, mercenaries are found in the
employ of a rebel baron, Robert of Bellême, and their
use became more frequent as the century wore on. The use
of the fyrd by the first three Norman kings also falls outside the accepted concept of feudalism. Indeed, there is
no evidence to suggest that the feudal kings of England
even attempted to meet their military needs from feudal
sources alone, and it would be impossible to cite an action
in which an army was composed only of feudal contingents. Nor can it be documented with any certainty that
there was ever a battle waged entirely by cavalry. The
quality of the troops available to Norman commanders
was sufficiently high to permit a considerable degree of
tactical flexibility, and fighting in post-Conquest England
never hardened into a stereotyped pattern.

5

Crusader Syria: A Feudal Military Frontier

On 15 July 1099 the warriors of the First Crusade completed the reduction of Jerusalem, thus achieving the goal for which they had set out from Europe some three years earlier. Less than a month later, the first Moslem counterattack against the Latins was crushed near Ascalon. The victory gave the Crusaders time to draw breath, and though years of fighting were still before them, the Franks were now in a position to consider how to hold and govern the occupied areas. Frankish authority had already been established in Edessa and Antioch; with the later addition of Tripoli, their control extended from the upper Euphrates to the borders of Egypt. But, with the exception of the county of Edessa, the Latin conquests nowhere penetrated very far inland, nor were the powerful Moslem principalities of Aleppo and Damascus reduced. The states established as a result of the First Crusade were always vulnerable to attack from the east, as well as from Egypt to the south.

Although the Frankish conquests in the Levant bear a superficial resemblance to the earlier Norman conquests in

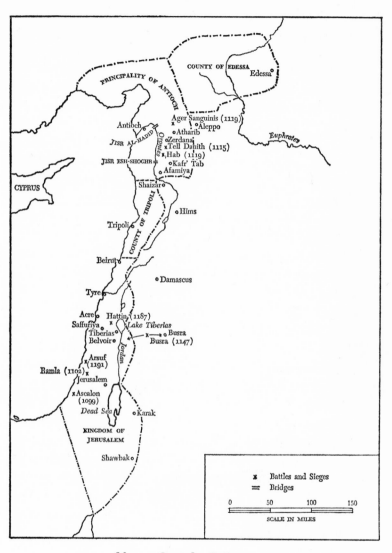

COUNTY OF EDESSA

Edessa

PRINCIPALITY OF ANTIOCH

Ager Sanguinis (1119)
× Aleppo
Antioch · Atharib
JISR AL-HADID
Zerdana
×Tell Danith (1115)
JISR ESH-SHOGHR Hab (1119)
Kafr' Tab
Afamiya
Euphrates

CYPRUS

Shaizar
COUNTY OF TRIPOLI
Hims
Tripoli

Beirut

Damascus

Tyre

Acre Hattin (1187)
Saffuriya ×
Tiberias Lake Tiberias
Belvoir × → Busra
Busra (1147)
Arsuf
×(1191)
Ramla (1102) ×
Jerusalem
×Ascalon
(1099)
Dead Sea Karak

KINGDOM OF
JERUSALEM

Shawbak

× Battles and Sieges
= Bridges

0   50   100   150
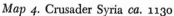
SCALE IN MILES

Map 4. Crusader Syria *ca.* 1130

Italy and England, there were significant differences. In both Italy and England traditions and institutions existed which the conquerors were able to adapt to their own purposes. With the exception of certain fiscal procedures, there were no native institutions in the east which could readily be adapted to Frankish needs. Except, perhaps, in the city of Edessa, a majority of the inhabitants were Moslems, ready, when occasion offered, to aid the enemy. The Christian minority were members of communions regarded by the Franks as schismatic at best; there was no possibility of forging an effective alliance—political and military—between church and state as William the Conqueror had in England a generation earlier. Moreover, the native Christians, who had been subjected to Moslem rule for more than 450 years, were, with few exceptions, unwarlike, and so far as can be determined, they seldom contributed significantly to the military resources of the Frankish states. Syria had nothing to compare with the English monarchy and its tradition of royal prerogative and the nucleus of a central administration, nor with the shadowy memory of Merovingian and Carolingian kingship in France that survived into Capetian times. Nor was there anything resembling the Byzantine organization which the Normans had found in Italy. It is not surprising, therefore, that the military and political organization of Crusader Syria differed in many significant ways from that of postconquest Italy and England. What emerged in the Crusader states has been described as "a society organized for war" and "the perfect feudal society." That the Frankish states in the Levant were organized for war cannot be doubted. Whether they constituted "a perfect feudal society" depends very largely on what is defined as feudal.

The kingship in the Latin east was the creation of Baldwin I (1100–1118). Although he occupied only the position of feudal overlord to the prince of Antioch and the counts of Edessa and Tripoli, Baldwin was able, by his military ability and sheer force of personality, to intervene effectively, especially in times of military crisis, in the affairs of his not always willing vassals. But as long as Moslem power in the Middle East was fragmented, it was possible for the Frankish states to preserve their position by mutual cooperation in which the king was the coordinating factor. Nevertheless, the king was only the first among peers. When, with the rise of Zanki (1127–1146) and Nur ed-Din (1146–1174), eventually the rulers of Moslem Syria, the threat to the Latin bridgehead in the Levant became continuous, each Frankish prince had to look to his own defenses. After the middle of the century the reunification of the Moslem east created a situation which the Franks simply had not the resources to counteract.

The principal weakness of the Christian states was a lack of manpower. Europeans did not emigrate to the east in sufficient numbers to assure an adequate defense of their conquests against determined Moslem counterattacks. Accurate figures are, of course, impossible to obtain, but it has been estimated that the short-lived county of Edessa never attracted more than 100 European noble and knightly families. Perhaps double that number settled permanently in the tiny county of Tripoli, which, under certain circumstances, owed 100 knights to the kingdom of Jerusalem. It can be surmised that the entire mounted service due the prince of Antioch amounted to about 700 knights. Again precise figures are lacking, but in 1119, the

Antiochene army, unsupported by contingents from any other Christian state, mustered about 700 knights. This must have represented very nearly the full levy of the principality. For the kingdom of Jerusalem there is late evidence which, however, reflects conditions during the reign of Baldwin IV (1174–1185). The distinguished Cypriot jurist John of Ibelin reckoned the total service due the kingdom of Jerusalem at about 675 knights, but this does not represent the maximum force available at the time of the kingdom's greatest extent. By Baldwin's time, some important fiefs had been permanently lost to the Moslems; there is no way of ascertaining the service due prior to their loss. The *servitia debita* ranged from 100 knights, due from each of the greatest baronies, down to the personal service rendered by individual knights holding in chief—that is, holding fiefs directly of the king. It may be a reasonable guess that the kingdom of Jerusalem, during the second quarter of the twelfth century, could, in a pinch, muster perhaps 1000 knights from normal feudal sources.[1]

In Latin Syria, the squadrons of mailed cavalry were the principal striking force available to Christian commanders. These formations would, however, have been absolutely useless had they not been supported by the infantry. Little is known of the infantry components of the Latin armies.

---

[1] The problem of mounted service due the Latin princes has been examined by almost everyone who has written on the subject. Of particular importance are the discussions in Steven Runciman, *A History of the Crusades* (3 vols.; Cambridge, 1951–1953), II, 291–292; John L. LaMonte, *Feudal Monarchy in the Latin Kingdom of Jerusalem, 1100–1291* (Cambridge, Mass., 1932), p. 147; and R. C. Smail, *Crusading Warfare (1097–1193)* (Cambridge, 1956), p. 89–90.

For the counties of Edessa and Tripoli, nothing whatever can be deduced from the surviving evidence. The prince of Antioch is said by a first-hand witness to have mustered some 3000 foot soldiers for the campaign of 1119, a figure that seems to be well within the bounds of probability. John of Ibelin stated that the king of Jerusalem could muster somewhat more than 5000 sergeants from obligated sources. The sergeanties seem not to have been of the same nature as the more familiar English tenures that men held in return for less than knightly military service. Contingents were due, not from individual tenants, but from ecclesiastical and urban communities. While not summoned for every campaign, they must have been called out fairly frequently. An army composed only of mounted troops was regarded as out of the ordinary. The discipline and steadiness displayed by Frankish infantry in many a campaign could not have been attained without some leaven of experienced soldiers.

The imprecise nature of the terms under which military quotas were imposed on the towns and ecclesiastical communities of the Latin kingdom serves only to emphasize the impossibility of neatly classifying medieval military practices. Were these quotas set arbitrarily, or was there some standard basis on which they were computed? If the former, it would be possible to agree with Smail's contention that in Jerusalem infantry service was as typical a feudal incident as was the knight service imposed upon the lay tenants-in-chief. But if quotas were determined by such factors as wealth, land, or population, it would be possible to see in the system strong similarities to the Old English fyrd.

In theory, then, the Latin king of Jerusalem could put

into the field from feudal and other obligated sources an army of perhaps 1,750–1,800 knights and about 10,000 infantry. There is no indication that the entire host of the Frankish states was ever assembled under a single banner. But even if it had been, and even though no limit was set on the length of service, such resources were obviously inadequate to preserve the Christian bridgehead in the Levant.

As the Moslem east became increasingly unified after about 1140, and as feudal service began to diminish because of loss of territory and the impoverishment of fiefs, the Latin rulers had to resort to a variety of expedients to augment normal sources of military manpower. The most obvious source, provided adequate financial means were available, was the mercenary. While mercenaries had been employed by the Latin kings since the reign of Baldwin I, the problem was always one of money. Special levies were imposed in 1124 and again in 1183 for the express purpose of paying mercenaries, both horse and foot; the evidence suggests that there was an increasing reliance on stipendiary troops as the century wore on.

Another source of military strength was the constant flow of pilgrims from Europe. This was especially important in the kingdom of Jerusalem, which contained the holy places of the Christian faith. The great expeditions commanded by monarchs or great nobles are well known, but many lesser magnates with armed followings, as well as individual knights, made the pilgrimage to the east. These pilgrims could be utilized in a variety of ways. The arrival of a large contingent usually led to an expedition against the Moslems. There were always knightly pilgrims who remained in Palestine to participate in a campaign or two before returning home. And in times of crisis, the

Latin rulers requisitioned fighting men wherever they could be found. In 1102, pilgrims waiting for their return passage at Jaffa were commandeered to help Baldwin I at the second battle of Ramla. Similarly, pilgrims were pressed into service in 1113 and 1153, and in 1183 they formed part of the greatest army ever mustered in the Latin east—that which confronted Saladin in the valley of Jezreel.

But mercenaries for whom payment could not be provided and pilgrims, whose numbers must have fluctuated greatly, could not provide a steady source of manpower to meet the military needs of the Frankish state. As the twelfth century advanced, these needs were met to an ever increasing extent by the contingents of the military orders of the Hospital of St. John of Jerusalem and the Knights of the Temple of Solomon. The orders of St. John and of the Temple, founded to serve the needs of pilgrims in the Holy Land, underwent rapid militarization during the second quarter of the twelfth century. Their contingents after about 1150 were a welcome addition to the military resources of the Latin kingdom. Precise figures are lacking as to the numbers of troops the orders could put into the field. A clue is offered by the agreement reached between King Amalric (1163–1174) and the Knights of St. John whereby, in return for immense territorial concessions, the order would supply a contingent of 500 knights and 500 turcopoles for the king's projected conquest of Egypt.[2]

[2] Turcopoles were light-armed cavalry, apparently recruited from among offspring of parents of different religions. They were often employed for reconnaissance purposes—not always skillfully. In line of battle they were marshaled with knights and thus augmented the always undermanned mounted squadrons. For a fuller discussion, see Smail, *Crusading Warfare*, pp. 111–112.

For this additional military strength the Latin kings paid a price, increasingly heavy as time went on. The military orders, responsible only to the Holy See, could not be fully controlled by any lay or ecclesiastical authority in the Frankish east. As a result, the Templars and Hospitalers took the field more as allies than as subordinates of the king of Jerusalem. The orders sought with great success to establish their right to pursue a military policy independent of the authority of any lay ruler in Latin Syria. If they declared war or negotiated a truce, the prince was obliged to observe it; conversely, a ruler might not conclude a truce that was opposed by the orders. Should he do so, they were not bound to observe it. It was universally regarded as a law of war that any plunder acquired during a campaign should be divided among all who had participated in the expedition; the orders sought and obtained the privilege of keeping everything they had taken. The contingents brought into the field by the military orders provided the Frankish princes with troops of excellent quality who partially offset the inadequacies of the feudal levy and the lack of financial resources for hiring sufficient mercenaries. In victory and defeat they played a distinguished, often heroic role during the last decades of the twelfth century. But as a result of the independence sought and obtained by the knights of St. John and the Temple, secular rulers lost the effective control of military policy and operations that had contributed so much to Frankish success earlier in the century.

The Franks had established themselves in Syria as conquerors; but they never held more than a bridgehead, which was subject to attack at any time, often from several directions simultaneously. This was a factor that rulers of more extensive European states did not have to consider seriously. A king of England faced with an invasion by the Scots could safely deplete garrisons in unthreatened districts to form a field army. As royal resources increased and were handled more efficiently, Philip Augustus of France could even maintain two field armies in 1214 to meet threats on his eastern and southern frontiers. Such options were not open to the Latin rulers of Syria. In time of war there were no interior areas which could be safely stripped of defenders to bolster a threatened frontier. European princes could also use diplomatic means to protect one frontier if another was attacked. Seldom were they forced to face invasions on all exposed fronts. Owing to a reluctance to negotiate with the infidel—although alliances were occasionally formed—diplomacy was seldom possible for the Frankish princes; after the unification of Moslem Syria and Egypt under Saladin, it became entirely impossible. The Frankish rulers of Syria were faced with a dilemma from which there was no escape.

The conquest and subsequent expansion in the early years of the twelfth century were due partly to the divisions and jealousies among the princes of Moslem Syria, but they were also the result of the careful management of inadequate military resources by Christian commanders whose skill and prudence deserve the admiration of all military writers. Frankish generals were hard-headed, practical fighting men who were able to adapt their thinking and their practices to cope with new problems, both strategic and tactical. While there was no conscious creation of a body of accepted military doctrine in the modern sense, there were military practices which were thoroughly understood and followed. In feudal Europe warfare was usually limited in scope and objective. All-or-nothing campaigns, such as that of Duke William of Normandy in 1066 or of Robert Guiscard against the Byzantine empire in 1085, were exceptions. Thus it required no great reorientation on the part of Christian commanders to adjust to warfare for limited objectives in Syria.

As in Europe, the prime goal of warfare was the acquisition or successful defense of fortified positions. If such an objective could be attained without incurring the risks of battle, so much the better. Victory in the open field could be important to an attacker to the extent that it left him free to pursue his plan to reduce the fortresses. For the defender, the all-important thing was to maintain an army in being. The presence of an army in the field served as a deterrent to the operations of an invader.

Battle could be risked only as a last resort or when the odds appeared to be overwhelmingly favorable. A pitched battle is almost always a gamble, even when every precaution has been taken to insure victory. In Latin Syria the prospect of casualties—either in killed or captured knights —must always have been prominent in the thoughts of commanders. Knights were precious commodities not lightly to be exposed to damage; their capture imposed an almost impossible burden on their tenants, who were required somehow to come up with ransom money. Defeat would place the all-important fortresses in double jeopardy. The field army had to be drawn from the garrisons of castles and walled towns; its destruction would enable the victorious enemy to turn his full attention and energy to the reduction of the undermanned strongholds. Under ordinary circumstances the rewards of possible victory were not attractive enough to warrant the risk of possible defeat.

Success in battle was vital to the Franks in the early decades of the twelfth century. But as Moslem Syria was gradually unified by Zanki, Nur ed-Din, and Saladin, a victory in the field yielded only temporary respite from Moslem pressure. These princes commanded sufficient resources to resume the offensive at the earliest favorable opportunity. Victory would end the campaign and effect the withdrawal of the invaders, but owing to the seasonal character of warfare in Syria, this result could have been achieved by waiting for the approach of winter and the inevitable breakup of the Moslem army which always accompanied the onset of cold, wet weather. In many instances what might have been achieved by a victory in the field was accomplished by means that did not risk the consequences of defeat. Recognition of these facts imposed a policy of caution upon Frankish commanders that is at odds with the generally accepted idea that feudal generals were invariably rash, impatient, and incapable of exercising restraint.

Operations without serious fighting might be called campaigns of maneuver. One of the most brilliant was the campaign of 1115, which combined a strategical defense with a tactical offense. Beginning in 1111, the Moslems had launched a series of annual attacks against the Franks in northern Syria. The Seljuk sultan in Baghdad seemed determined to drive out the intruders, but he experienced much difficulty in securing the cooperation of the princes of Moslem Syria, who felt that their positions would be threatened by any extension of the sultan's authority.

Hence, when the sultan appointed Bursuq ben Bursuq, the ruler of Hamadan, to command an expedition against the Christians in 1115, the Syrian Moslems allied themselves with the Franks.

Prince Roger of Antioch took immediate steps to meet the invasion threat. In the spring of 1115, Roger was personally directing the repair of the castles damaged by the great earthquake of November 1114, especially those which stood closest to the Moslem frontier. At the same time he summoned the levy of the principality to muster at Jisr al-Hadid, where a bridge spanned the Orontes a dozen miles northeast of Antioch. Agents were sent into Mesopotamia to observe enemy movements, and Antioch was put in a proper state of defense. Meanwhile, supplies were forwarded to the army, and Roger joined his troops at Jisr al-Hadid, where he received intelligence that the sultan had indeed decided to invade Syria. After consultation with his commanders, Roger marched his army to Atharib, on the main Antioch–Aleppo road. Here an agreement was reached between Prince Roger and the Moslem rulers of Damascus, Mardin, and Aleppo to join in resistance to the sultan's army. It was decided to avoid battle and to trust that Bursuq's army would break up at the approach of winter. The allies then concentrated their forces at Afamiya, in the Orontes Valley, which became the forward base for operations. It was well supplied and reasonably secure; it was close enough to Hims and Shaizar to discourage their rulers from openly supporting Bursuq, and its central location would enable the allies to march directly to repel any attack on Aleppo, Antioch, or Damascus.

Bursuq's movements soon showed the wisdom of the

choice of Afamiya as a base. The Moslem commander
took Hama by storm and then marched to Shaizar. Contact was made at once between the invaders and Prince
Roger and his allies. The Moslems made the usual attempts to provoke the Latins into an ill-considered attack,
but to no avail. As soon as he was certain that Bursuq had
invaded Syria, Prince Roger had requested aid from King
Baldwin I and Count Pons of Tripoli. On the day he received Roger's message, Baldwin sent off a dispatch to the
count of Tripoli directing him to be prepared to march
with the army of Jerusalem to the aid of the Antiochenes.
In addition, strict instructions were sent to the prince not
to engage the enemy until the arrival of the combined
forces of Jerusalem and Tripoli.[3] It is recorded that for the
campaign Roger had mustered some 2000 knights and infantry; Baldwin I marched with 500 knights and 1000 infantry, to which were added 200 knights and 2000 foot
soldiers brought in by Count Pons. The contingents of the
Moslem princes are said to have numbered 5000, and the
total of 10,700 men does not seem an impossible figure.
The king's instructions were followed to the letter, but
even before the arrival of the reinforcements under King
Baldwin, Bursuq had been informed of their approach. He
broke up his camp at Shaizar and marched away to the
east. To all appearances another invasion of Syria had
been repelled. The allied army, lulled into a false sense of
security, broke up, and the components, under their re-
spective princes, returned home.

[3] Much has been written about the shadowy nature of the overlordship exercised by the kings of Jerusalem over the other Frankish princes. During the first half of the twelfth century there was
nothing shadowy about their supremacy. Baldwin could issue
directives to the prince of Antioch and expect to be obeyed.

In view of Roger's carefully organized intelligence service, it is difficult to understand why all contact with Bursuq was lost, but no sooner had the allied army dissolved than he reappeared, captured Kafr' Tab, and made threatening movements in the direction of Zerdana. On receiving this unwelcome news, Roger immediately recalled his levies, marched south from Antioch, and crossed the Orontes at Jisr esh-Shoghr, some thirty miles south of the city. Here he was in a position to fall back, if necessary, on the castle of Rugia a few miles to the rear and at the same time pose a threat to the flank of Bursuq's army marching across his front in the direction of Zerdana. On 14 September, Roger received intelligence that the Moslems, apparently unaware of the near presence of a Frankish army, were going into camp at a water point near Tell Danith, in the valley of Sarmin. Roger lost no time in taking the initiative. On the same day he attacked Bursuq's army as it was still in the process of making camp, achieved complete surprise, and won a decisive victory.

The campaign of 1115 is instructive in a number of respects. It illustrates, for one thing, the capabilities of Frankish generals during the best days of the Crusader states. By pursuing a strictly defensive policy, the allies had prevented Bursuq from making any significant gains. When the invader suddenly reappeared, Prince Roger was able to capitalize on his intelligence and achieve complete tactical surprise. The enemy was sent in disorganized flight back to Mesopotamia, and the Frankish victory near Tell Danith marked the end of the attempts of the Seljuk sultans to drive the Crusaders out of Syria.

It is also important to note the duration of the campaign. The Antiochene levies had been called out in the spring and remained long enough at Jisr al-Hadid to accumulate the supplies necessary for the expected operations. To this time must be added the interval necessary for the marches to Atharib and subsequently to Afamiya, and a two month's encampment at the latter place. There followed an attack on Shaizar, the return march to Antioch, the dispersal of the army, and its recall within a short time for the operations culminating in the battle near Tell Danith on 14 September. It is known that Bursuq's forces began to move westward in February; how soon after that time Roger called out the host of Antioch is unknown, but it seems likely that it was at least five months before the Antiochene forces were finally mustered out sometime after the middle of September. A campaign of this duration was a heavy burden on the military tenants and a striking contrast to the limited obligations already customary in much of western Europe.

Later in the century, as the Moslem east was gradually unified, first under Nur ed-Din and then under Saladin, the necessity for avoiding battle, except in the most favorable or in the most desperate situations, became overriding. The campaign of 1182 illustrates the predicament which faced the Latin kings. On 11 May of that year, Saladin left Egypt at the head of an army, marching toward Damascus by way of Ai'la and the desert route. As soon as the direction of the Moslem advance was known, King Baldwin IV summoned a council to determine a plan of campaign. At once two factions emerged, each arguing for a different course of action. Basic to the argument was the conflict between feudal custom and sound strategy. Feudal custom demanded that a lord march to defend a fief attacked by the Moslems, and the territory through which Saladin was marching formed part of the fiefs of Karak and Shawbak (Montreal). One party in the council urged that the field army take up a position beyond Jordan to defend the threatened territory. The other faction pointed out that to move the field army east of the Jordan would be virtually to strip the kingdom of troops. The council, however, decided to march into Transjordan. By occupying Petra, King Baldwin hoped to prevent the capture of the castles on which control of the lordship depended, as well as to protect the crops which were white for the harvest (John 4:35). Saladin's line of march was, of course, determined by the water points along the western edge of the desert. If the Franks could have denied him the use of these, he would have been forced out into the desert and away from the cultivated lands. This they were unable to do.

Meanwhile, Saladin's campaign had been going well. He was aware of the military dilemma of the Franks, and he had the resources to exploit their weakness to the full. Knowing that virtually the entire levy of the Latin kingdom was required to confront the main Moslem army, he launched diversionary attacks which the Franks were unable to oppose. It proved impossible, however, for Saladin to achieve any of the normal objectives of a campaign, so he resorted to destructive raids on the open countryside. Because of the marginal capacity of the Franks to resist aggression, any diminuation of their material resources was bound to affect adversely their ability to organize an adequate defense. Saladin established a base at the water point at Jerba, and from there detachments ravaged the croplands of Montreal (Shawbak). Simultaneously, Galilee was raided and extensively plundered by Saladin's nephew, Farrukh Shah, the commander at Damascus. In the first phase of the campaign the Franks had preserved their essential fortresses without exposing the field army to the hazards of a pitched battle, but local damage must have been extensive.

Toward the middle of June, Saladin broke off contact with the Franks and marched away to Damascus, which he reached on the twenty-second. But in less than three weeks (11 July) he again took the field, encamping at Al-Quhwana, at the southern end of the lake of Tiberias, and again sending detachments to harry the countryside. He then crossed the Jordan, marching southeastward along the high ground between Lake Tiberias and Baisan on which stood the new castle of Belvoir (Kawkab al-Hawa). In the meantime the Frankish field army, returning from beyond the Jordan, had concentrated at Suffuriya, a castle about six miles northwest of Nazareth. In the generation before 1187, this fortress was the usual base from which defensive operations were conducted in northern Palestine. It was admirably located for the purpose, having an ample supply of water and excellent communications with Acre and the coastal plain. From Suffuriya the Latin army could make immediate contact with an invader who crossed the Jordan either north or south of Lake Tiberias.

When reconnaissance gave some indication of Saladin's movements, a decision was made to establish contact at once with the enemy. The army was strengthened by stripping all available troops from the garrisons of nearby castles. The Franks then marched from Suffuriya to Tiberias, thence south along the Jordan, finally moving to the high ground in the vicinity of Kawkab. Here they spent the night in a heavily guarded bivouac and on the following morning found themselves in the presence of the enemy. The march was resumed, and a typical running engagement resulted. The Moslems attempted to bring the column to a halt and force a general action; the Latins resolutely preserved their tight formation and continued the march. Skirmishing was heavy throughout the day, but there was no pitched battle. Finding that he could obtain no decisive strategic or tactical results, Saladin broke off contact and marched back to Damascus.

The campaigning season, however, was not yet over, and the feudal tenants of the kingdom of Jerusalem and the mercenaries in the king's pay could not yet be dismissed. Saladin now moved to attack Beirut in cooperation with a fleet from Egypt. When lookouts posted in the Lebanon reported sighting the ships, Saladin marched from Damascus, crossed the mountains by the Munaitira Pass, and attacked the town. At the same time detachments from Egypt launched a diversionary invasion of southern Palestine. Once again the Frankish army concentrated at Suffuriya under the command of King Baldwin. Marching to Tyre, the king requisitioned all available shipping, with the intention of relieving Beirut. When Saladin learned of Baldwin's activities, he raised the siege, withdrew from Frankish territory, and the campaign of 1182 finally ended. These operations illustrate vividly the arduous nature of military service in the Latin kingdom in the years immediately before the disaster at Hattin (1187). A single mistake on the part of a Frankish commander could lose the field army, the fortresses, and with them the whole kingdom.

The Latin princes limited their strategy, after the initial period of expansion, to defending their conquests. Military conditions dictated that their scanty resources in man-power be carefully husbanded, that unless absolutely nec-essary, military objectives be obtained by other means than battle. In the realm of tactics, however, the Crusad-ers from the very outset found it necessary to modify the ideas which they brought with them from Europe. After the near disaster at Dorylaeum (1 July 1097) it must have been obvious to the leaders of the First Crusade that tradi-tional tactics could not cope with the methods employed by their new enemies, the Seljuk Turks. The Turks were horsemen, but man to man they were no match for the more heavily mounted, more heavily armored Europeans. The problem for the Europeans was how to come to grips with an enemy who was far more mobile than any foe the westerners had had to face since the Magyars, more than a century earlier.

The Turks usually opened their attack at bowshot range, keeping up a steady flight of arrows, hoping by these harassing tactics to produce one of two results. The enemy might be provoked into a premature charge, which the more agile Turks could easily evade, or the foe's marching order might loosen, and the Turks could themselves charge in with lance and sword to exploit the gaps. The problem of the crusading commanders was to devise a formation that would be flexible enough to offer resistance on the march and that, in line of battle, would be able to maintain its solidity until the Turks had so far committed themselves that the ponderous charge of the mailed knights would be decisive.

Smail gives almost total credit for the development of a tactical system which would meet these requirements to Bohemund of Taranto, whom he regards as the only leader of the First Crusade to emerge as a skillful general.[4] This assessment gives too much credit to Bohemund, who despite his considerable abilities contrived to get himself captured by the Turks in 1100 and was twice defeated by the Byzantine emperor Alexius I. Although he was not present at the battles which decided the fate of Antioch, the commander who did most to consolidate Frankish rule in Syria was King Baldwin I, to whom the military organization of the Christian states owes much. The chief characteristic of the tactical formation evolved by Frankish commanders was the close cooperation of infantry and cavalry. But no less important, and less frequently remarked, was the high standard of discipline maintained. This was absolutely essential, since the mobility of the Turks enabled them to attack from any or all sides. Thus every man was assigned a position in the line of march and was strictly forbidden to leave it. Usually the infantry, armed with bows and spears, occupied the position nearest the enemy, with the knights riding in the center of the column. On occasion, if the Turks pressed too closely on flanks or rear, the knights would charge out to drive the enemy to a safer distance, making sure not to incur the risk of being cut off and surrounded.

The effectiveness of this procedure was dramatically proven during the campaign of 1147. In that year the emir of Busra and Salkhad, at odds with his suzerain in Damascus, offered to turn the two towns over to the Latins. Busra and Salkhad lie on the western edge of the desert some sixty-five miles southeast of Damascus and are less than fifteen miles apart. An expedition to take possession of the towns would certainly meet determined opposition

[4] Smail, *Crusading Warfare*, p. 202.

from the Damascene army, aided by Nur ed-Din, the ambitious ruler of Mosul and Aleppo. Soon after the Frankish army began its march under the command of King Baldwin III (1143–1163), the Turks appeared in heavy force. Resisting the temptation to offer battle, the Latin commanders pitched camp, around which a careful watch was maintained to prevent a surprise attack. The following morning a council of war decided to continue the march to Busra. In order to maintain the solidity of the column, the pace of the mounted troops was made to conform to that of the infantry. To constant harassment by the Turks, to which the Franks could reply only with archery, was added the torture of thirst. It required four days to reach the vicinity of Busra, where water and supplies could be obtained. But it was then learned that the emir's wife, obviously a lady of determined character, had admitted a garrison of Damascene troops into the citadel, and there was no choice but to retreat.

The return march was far more difficult than the advance. The Franks were harassed by constant Turkish attacks in addition to the normal discomforts of a campaign —heat, dust, and the thirst of a Syrian summer. On one occasion the Turks fired the dry brush upwind of the column so that the Christian army had also to endure the flame and acrid smoke. The Turks, however, were never able to bring the Frankish column to a halt, and it maintained its steady progress with its ranks tightly closed. Lest the enemy be encouraged by knowledge of casualties he had inflicted, the wounded and the bodies of the slain were carried along with the column. The strictest orders were issued that no man should leave his place in the ranks. As the Latin army approached the frontiers of the kingdom of Jerusalem, Turkish assaults were intensified on the rear elements in the hope of either cutting them off from the rest of the army or of compelling the entire column to come to a halt. These attempts were unsuccessful. The Franks reached friendly territory, and the army was demobilized after having maintained itself for twelve days against the almost constant attacks of a determined enemy.

Although the campaign of 1147 was a complete failure from a practical standpoint, King Baldwin and his subordinate commanders must have looked back on the Busra expedition with considerable satisfaction. Their army had been subjected to the heaviest hostile pressure as well as the normal wear and tear of a campaign in the not too friendly environment of a Syrian summer, and they had acquitted themselves well.

Far too little credit is given to the organization and discipline of the Frankish armies in Syria. While there is no mention of anything like regular training, it is likely that the almost annual campaigns would have provided a kind of on-the-job training for the survivors. Especially impressive was the ability of the Franks to maintain formation while literally marching through the enemy. Such a running fight took place in twelfth-century England at Winchester in 1141, but there the entire retreating column came apart, its commander was captured in a desperate rear-guard action, and the army ceased to exist as a fighting force.

Until recently the attention of military historians was focused almost exclusively on the pitched battles. In fact, not a great deal is known about either the order of battle or the tactical expedients relied upon by the Latins in

Syria. Most surviving accounts lack the detail necessary for an accurate reconstruction of battlefield maneuvers. It may be concluded, however, that tactics were simple, although on two occasions there is mention of the use of the feigned flight—apparently under controlled conditions. But there is no other suggestion of tactical novelties. The application of ordinary common sense to battlefield conditions seems to have been the guiding factor.[5] The role of the field army during the initial phase of conquest and occupation was to extend and consolidate Frankish territory by the capture of Moslem fortresses. After the rise of Zanki and the loss of Edessa, except in the significant attempt by King Amalric I to gain control of Egypt (1163–1169), the primary function of the field army was to interfere with Moslem attempts to take Frankish fortified places. Many campaigns ended without a general action, but battle was always a possibility. There is some evidence that a rather standard order of battle evolved. When a general action was sought or seemed inevitable, it was customary to subdivide the army into smaller units and to form them in battle order in a prearranged pattern. Depending, doubtless, on the numbers available, the mounted troops were divided into five or six squadrons whose strength seems to have varied between 100 and 150. It was also a common practice to brigade the squadrons into three divisions: right, center, and left. Sometimes

---

[5] Smail discusses in considerable detail the possible extraneous influences on Frankish military practices in Syria—classical and Byzantine. Although there were numerous Byzantine contacts— occasional joint campaigns were conducted in Asia Minor—he regards the argument as not proven (*Crusading Warfare*, pp. 121–123).

a reserve under the personal control of the field commander was also provided.[6] The army was not always organized into three divisions; the Franks went into the battle of Ascalon (August 1099) with the army divided into nine squadrons deployed on a front of three squadrons, three squadrons deep. It may be surmised that at this early date the Latin tactical formation had not yet evolved into its final form.

Milites peditesque—"horse and foot"—is the customary description of Frankish armies by contemporary chroniclers. While Latin commanders relied on the charge of the mailed horsemen to produce victory, these were usually covered by an infantry screen until the decisive moment, since cavalry are not very effective on the defensive. How the infantry were organized is unknown, but apparently the archers and spearmen were posted in front of the knights during the first stages of a battle. Their mission was to hold off the enemy until the commander decided that it was time to send the horse into action.

None of these preaction measures was a complete innovation. William of Normandy had devised an order of battle at Hastings in which the action was opened by the infantry. Had European commanders possessed regular troops with a permanent organization, such battlefield subdivision and marshaling would have been unnecessary.

[6] Smail states that the deployment of a tactical reserve under the command of the general who did not join in the fight at first was a normal medieval practice, although he gives no examples (*Crusading Warfare*, p. 170). There were occasions when this procedure was followed, of course, but they were exceptional. It can be fairly well established that the medieval general usually put all his troops in line or in column of divisions and fought in the front rank himself.

But in the twelfth century, when every army differed in composition and personnel from every other there was no alternative. It thus became necessary to subdivide the available troops into manageable units. Only in this way could a commander issue orders and retain control of the army. Once the order to charge had been given, he could no longer influence the course of the action.

Efforts to discover consistent tactical practices in Frankish Syria have been unrewarded, probably because no such consistency can be found either in feudal or any other times. It can be shown that for a pitched battle Latin armies at times attacked with squadrons in line abreast when it was necessary to cover as broad a front as possible. On other occasions the mounted troops attacked with the squadrons in echelon. Thus it would appear that Frankish commanders and Frankish armies in Syria, like their feudal counterparts elsewhere, were capable of making more than a stereotyped response to a given tactical situation.

The "typical" feudal battle is as difficult to discover as the "typical" feudal manor, and for the same reasons. No two manors were alike; neither were any two battles. But while all sorts of documents have survived regarding the size, population, and economic resources of manors throughout western Europe, the same, unfortunately, is not true of battles. Only occasionally was one described by a competent eyewitness. One such was the battle of Hab, fought 14 August 1119. On 28 June of that year, the same Prince Roger of Antioch who had conducted the brilliant campaign of 1115 had allowed himself to be surprised and trapped by Il Ghazi of Mardin in a valley with steep wooded sides. In the resulting action, the Antiochene army, said to have numbered 700 knights and 3000 infantry, was virtually destroyed. Prince Roger was among the slain. So indelible was the memory of this disaster that the Frankish chroniclers thereafter always referred to it as *Ager Sanguinis,* "the Field of Blood."

The news of the death of Prince Roger and the destruction of his army brought King Baldwin II of Jerusalem (1118–1130) posthaste into northern Syria. On the way he seems to have picked up Count Pons of Tripoli and the contingent due from his county. Within a month of Roger's death the king was in Antioch. Here he rallied the remnants of the Antiochene army and prepared to take the field. In the meantime Il Ghazi had laid siege to Zerdana, about forty miles east-southeast of Antioch, in an attempt to reap some profit from his victory. King Baldwin marched from Antioch to raise the siege of Zerdana, but while he was encamped on Tell Danith, he learned that the town had fallen to the Moslems.

On receiving this news, the king decided to fall back on Hab, about fifteen miles southwest of Zerdana. Anticipating that the withdrawal would be opposed, he carefully organized the order of march, which must have been on a rather broad front through open country. The advanced element consisted of three squadrons of knights who may have been part of the Jerusalem component. These were followed by a column which included all the infantry levies. On the right flank was posted Count Pons with the Tripolitan knights; the left flank was guarded by Antiochene knights commanded by Robert Fulcoy. The rear elements consisted of additional squadrons from Antioch. The king marched with a reserve which could go to the relief of any threatened sector, but his precise location in the formation is not stated.

As soon as the march began, at dawn on 14 August, Turkish pressure was felt; the column, attacked from all sides with archery and other missiles, must soon have been brought to a halt. The Turks seem to have created or found a gap between the leading mounted squadrons and the infantry, for the foot soldiers were subjected to heavy attack. While they maintained their usual stubborn resistance, the rout of the three leading cavalry units deprived them of normal support, and they suffered heavy casualties. On the right, Robert Fulcoy defeated the forces immediately to his front, but after the pursuit, he did not return to the field. Instead he took his squadrons off to see what might be done about recapturing his castle at Zerdana which Il Ghazi had just taken. On the left, the contingent of Count Pons had been destroyed as an organized force. Many of his knights were soon in full flight, spreading news of a Christian defeat as far as Hab, Antioch, and even Tripoli itself. The count and a few of his knights were driven in on the squadrons commanded by the king, and here they continued to fight. It was indeed fortunate that King Baldwin had retained a reserve under his personal command. By his skill and energy and by his intervention at threatened points, he was able to maintain resistance. Owing to his efforts, the Turks eventually retired, and the Latins remained in possession of the field of battle.

The hard-won Frankish victory at Hab may not be typical of the pitched battles of the twelfth century, but it does illustrate the ingredients that were necessary to produce success under adverse circumstances. At Hab there was no decisive charge of the mailed knights, as there was at Ascalon in 1099 and at Sarmin in 1115. Hard fighting, skillful use of the available troops, and good leadership—these have always been major ingredients in the prescription for successful military operations. When they are lacking, disaster is the likely result.

It has been argued that the Crusaders deliberately created an elaborate system of defense along the frontier, but castles in the eleventh and twelfth centuries were never effective deterrents to an invading army. They were useful as centers of administration; they were frequently helpful in curbing border raids; their garrisons contributed the detachments that made up the field army. Above all, no area could be permanently occupied as long as its castles held out. These were the major functions of the castles and fortified towns, not the defense of a frontier. Indeed, there were long and strategically important stretches of the Christian frontier that were virtually undefended. Some castles were constructed on sites that more accurately reflected former Moslem and Byzantine frontiers. Still others were erected during the period of conquest and dominated districts that as yet had no definable frontier.

Nevertheless, the border strongholds had a special importance. Because of their proximity to the enemy, they were subject to frequent attack. When it was decided to meet an invader near the frontier, the castles served as bases, depots, and as refuges for the field army. All this is well put by Smail, who points out that no matter where it stood, the castle "was the embodiment of force, and therefore the ultimate sanction of the Latin Settlement." [7]

Frankish rule in the Levant was always precarious. It could have been made permanent only by the settlement of large numbers of Christians in the conquered territories or by continuous military support from the west. Some settlement there was, as well as some military aid, but there was never enough of either. So the rulers, who were also the military commanders of Latin Syria, had to make do with what they had. The local populations were of little help. Native Christians were unwarlike as a result of centuries of Moslem rule and were usually regarded by the Franks as schismatics at best. The sympathies of the Moslem population lay, naturally, with their former rulers, whom they were only too willing to aid when the opportunity offered.

So long as the Moslem east was politically fragmented, Frankish commanders, by a display of skill and energy—and great good luck—were able to preserve their foothold on the Syrian coast. Castles were built, the princes acted in close cooperation, and a modification of feudal military practice was worked out that enabled the Latins to meet successfully the tactics of new enemies. The Franks were fortunate in that the kings of Jerusalem before the final incapacitation of Baldwin IV in 1183 were men of energy and no little military ability. They were able to intervene when crises arose in the other Crusader states; there is little evidence to show that the kings did not exercise full and effective authority over their commands, even when operating beyond the strict confines of the kingdom. But above all, the Latin kings were cau-

[7] *Crusading Warfare*, p. 215.

tious men. They husbanded their limited manpower resources and seldom took unnecessary risks. This required the imposition of a discipline and self-restraint for which they have not always received due credit. Only when the Moslems of Syria and Egypt were united under Saladin did the situation in Frankish Syria become untenable.

The battle of Hattin only served to hasten the inevitable. On 3 July 1187, a Frankish column that included almost the full levy of the kingdom was marching to the relief of the citadel of Tiberias, then besieged by Saladin. The usual running fight developed between the Christian and Moslem armies, but this time the Latin column was brought to a halt short of Tiberias—and water. After a night during which the Frankish encampment was subject to continual harassment from all sides, the Moslems attacked the thirst-tortured and now demoralized enemy 4 July and virtually destroyed the military power of the Latin kingdom.

Military historians, by concentrating their attention on battles, have tended to overlook the truly remarkable achievements of the Latins in warfare as a whole. The wonder is not that the Franks eventually succumbed to a united Moslem east, but that they were able to hold on as long as they did. The tenacious stand, long after the odds had become insuperable, is a tribute to the ability and skill of Frankish commanders and to the fighting qualities of their men, *milites peditesque.*

6

Warfare in Southern France and Christian Spain

A clear distinction must be made between the southern and northern regions of France prior to the thirteenth century. South of the Loire older traditions and institutions survived with greater vigor, especially forms of landholding. As has been previously emphasized, landholding in the north became inseparably bound up with military service. But as late as the middle of the eleventh century, most land in southern France was still held in allodial tenure, and the holders were not necessarily the men of any lord. Only a small fraction of the land was held as fiefs in return for military service. In this respect, southern France bore more resemblance to Christian Spain than to the feudal states developing north of the Loire. With the passage of time, the number of grants in return for military service tended to increase, but allodial property continued to be a significant factor in the Midi. This in turn explains in large measure the inability of the greater magnates of the south to create the sort of centralized feudal states that emerged, for example, in Flanders and Normandy.

Although the lands of southern France, with the exception of Septimania, had been considered part of the Merovingian state, they continued for the most part to retain their Gallo-Roman laws and institutions. There were counts in Aquitaine and the Narbonnaise who, like their Carolingian successors, commanded the local armed forces during wartime, but little can be said about the composition of these forces or on what basis they were raised. Probably all free men were liable for military service, and the evidence suggests that the arms-bearing class was not so well organized as were the Frankish *vassi* under the first Carolingians. Indeed it is likely that the military resources of Aquitaine and Provence were inadequate to meet any major outside threat. When the Carolingians overran the Rhone Valley (736–739), they found that the patrician of Provence, Maurontius, had garrisoned his cities with Moslem mercenary troops, presumably because he found local levies either inadequate or unreliable. Similarly, there are frequent references to Gascons serving in the armies and garrisons of the dukes of Aquitaine. These auxiliary units probably were mercenaries employed to counter a threat that could not be met with ordinary military resources.

With regard to pre-Carolingian fortifications, the available information is more adequate. In the early eighth century the major cities of Provence were well fortified, as were the principal *civitates* of Septimania and Aquitaine. In addition to the fortified towns, *castella*, located outside the cities, are mentioned as early as 678; at least some of them were controlled by the counts within whose jurisdiction they were situated. Considering the looseness with which the chroniclers used the term *castellum* to describe anything from a fortified enclosure to a walled town, it would be unwise to speculate on the nature of such strongholds until more definitive archaeological research has been done in this area.

The revitalization of the Frankish state by the first Carolingians had surprisingly little impact on the conservative society of the Midi. Whenever possible, the new rulers made alliances with the magnates in the south, but otherwise military force was applied, Frankish officials were placed in authority, and Frankish garrisons were installed in many castles. Aquitaine occupied a unique position, for Charlemagne made it a subkingdom which was used as a training ground for royal heirs down to 828. Real authority, however, continued to be exercised by the counts who were responsible for local defense and the maintenance of the fortresses and who, in time of war, commanded the ban, the levy of all free men of a county. But in spite of the widespread appointment of Frankish officials and the construtcion of many new castles in which Frankish garrisons were installed, the Carolingians from the beginning relied heavily on non-Frankish *milites* and warriors to carry out their military policies. The expedition of 801–802, noted earlier, which invaded Catalonia and captured Barcelona was composed, besides the Frankish contingents, of Provençals under Count Leibulf, Aquitanians, Gascons commanded by Duke Lupo, and Goths under Count Bera. Furthermore, the Franks seem not to have introduced the military benefice to any significant extent.

The Frankish administration did, however, make one important innovation in the system of land tenure. This was the *aprisio*, a grant of waste land to individuals who were willing to put it into cultivation. *Aprisiones* had originally been granted to Christian refugees from Moorish Spain, but the system was soon extended to others, particularly in Catalonia after its reconquest in the early ninth century. In return for the *aprisio,* grantees, both great and small, assumed certain responsibilities, the most important of which was military service. These holders, sometimes referred to as *milites,* were required, when summoned, to join their count's army for service in frontier campaigns. At first glance there seems to be little difference between the holder of an *aprisio* and the *vassus dominicus* who held a military benefice. The benefice in the eighth and most of the ninth centuries, however, was a revocable grant, dependent on the satisfactory performance of military service. The holder of an *aprisio* enjoyed complete control of his grant, which he could sell, exchange, or will to his heirs. And just as during the late ninth and tenth centuries the benefice became a hereditary fief, so the *aprisio* became an allod, and was just as effectively removed from government control.

When the Carolingian state began to come apart in the later years of Louis the Pious (814–840), viable institutions of government all but disappeared in the Midi, where Frankish control had never been firmly secured. To civil disturbances were added Viking and Moslem raids, which the authorities seemed powerless to check. One chronicler, in fact, noted that during one period of particularly severe Viking incursions (845–852) the Aquitanian nobles were so busy fighting each other that they had no time to defend the land against the raiders.

There is very little specific evidence concerning the military system then in use. The Carolingian monarchs, as long as they exercised any authority in the Midi, regularly summoned their *fideles*—the counts, the *vassi dominici,* and the holders of the larger *aprisiones*—while the counts summoned their own *vassi.* It may also be assumed that if the capitularies of Charlemagne and his successors were enforced in the south of France, these contingents contained an increasing proportion of mounted troops as the century wore on. But almost nothing is known of how they were mustered or how they fought. There are numerous references to military actions of one sort or another, but the accounts lack the details from which an accurate picture of the post-Carolingian military organization might be reconstructed. One fact, however, emerges clearly: whatever the system, it was not very effective. The fighting men of the Midi seem to have been deficient in both organization and leadership. In the period from 828 to 900, no army from the south of France won a significant victory.

By the middle of the eleventh century certain states had emerged north of the Loire which were characterized by relatively effective control of feudal institutions by the immediate overlord. In the Midi, with a single exception, this control had not been possible, primarily because of the persistence in southern France of allodial property and the reluctance not only of owners of allods but also of the recipients of benefices to be brought into a truly feudal relationship with the nominal authority. By 975 there were some 150 families in southern France of comital or vicecomital standing who held *de facto* authority by hereditary right.

These rights were exercised and enforced by an extraordinary proliferation of castles, garrisoned by a new class of professional *milites.* Ecclesiastical magnates, as well as the lay nobility, owned and maintained numerous fortresses. Some strongholds were built with obvious military functions in mind, as were those that guarded the Alpine passes into Italy. The threat of Viking and Moslem attack was a factor in the construction of others. But for many there can have been no other justification than the necessity to hold a certain area which probably had been forcibly acquired. To garrison these castles a new military class evolved which had no parallel north of the Loire. The *milites* of the tenth and eleventh centuries in southern France differed from both their Carolingian predecessors and their contemporaries in northern France, who were becoming in reality a part-time obligated militia. The southern variety were professional fighters primarily, though they could be found serving in other capacities. Their homes were castles, which steadily increased in number throughout the period.

These *milites* seem to have been recruited from the ranks of minor officials and even from the servile class. Some landowners were compelled to threaten serfs who made themselves into *milites* and went about armed with lance and spear. The phrase "armed with lance and spear" at once suggests that in southern France, as elsewhere, the term *miles* did not, in the early eleventh century, mean specifically a heavy-armed horsemen, and it is likely that the garrisons of the castles of the Midi contained both horse and foot. To provide a living for these garrisons, special dues were levied on the inhabitants of the surrounding countryside.

By the middle of the eleventh century, castle ownership was being fragmented much as political authority had been during the break-up of the Carolingian state. Originally castles were the allodial property of holders both lay and ecclesiastical. For those magnates who possessed more than one such fortress, custodial problems were sometimes solved by a system of joint ownership (*divisio*) in which half the castle belonged to the occupant, and half to an owner who lived elsewhere. This led inevitably to fragmentation of ownership, as each half could be subdivided among heirs. Another abortive measure to retain ownership was to grant the castle to the castellan as a fief or benefice—a system adopted widely throughout the Midi and in Catalonia. It was, regardless of terminology, very different from true feudal tenure. The holder in England, for example, never granted any rights in a castle itself to his castellan. A castellan was generally a vassal, but for a fief in land; there were also some hereditary castellans, but they possessed no property rights in the castle. As might be expected, castles held as fiefs tended to become the allodial property of the occupant, and fragmentation of property rights soon appeared.

Thus by the middle of the eleventh century, although society in the Midi had changed in many ways, it was still based primarily on the allodial ownership of land, and despite a trend toward militarization, it could by no means be called a feudal society. Feudal tenure was not yet applied to the raising of military forces, and in only one area—Languedoc—did the amount of land held feudally exceed 10 per cent of the total, but the movement toward a more feudalistic society continued to grow in importance and to become more widespread during the remainder of the century.

One indication of the feudalistic trend is to be found in the rising fortunes of the counts of Poitou. Although there was little difference initially between the count of Poitou and his fellows in the struggle for supremacy that characterized the post-Carolingian era, he did have certain advantages. For one thing, he had managed to maintain a reasonable facsimile of a centralized Carolingian-type administration in his patrimonial lands. About the beginning of the eleventh century, he began to introduce feudal institutions modeled on those of adjacent Anjou and nearby Normandy. Thus the count had a relatively well-organized base from which to encroach on the lands of his vulnerable neighbors. At the head of armies supplied by his vassals, and with the aid of the counts of Anjou, he had, by about 1030, conquered most of the Limousin and had extended his control over Saintonge. By mid-century the erstwhile counts of Poitou were supreme north of the Garonne; when in 1053 they obtained Gascony, they became rulers of the great duchy of Aquitaine, extending from the Pyrenees to the Loire. It would be misleading, however, to regard the duchy of Aquitaine as a true feudal principality like Norman England, Flanders, or Anjou. In many regions the authority of the duke was but nominal. Even a century later, such able dukes of Aquitaine as Henry II and Richard I, who were also kings of England, found it impossible to fit the nobles of the Midi into the molds of English tenants-in-chief.

Christian Spain, until early in the thirteenth century, can be most accurately described as a military frontier, but owing to their historical experiences, the various kingdoms developed quite different military institutions and practices. In the northwest, the kingdom of Asturias and Galicia, cut off from direct contact with the rest of western Christendom for the better part of a century, retained

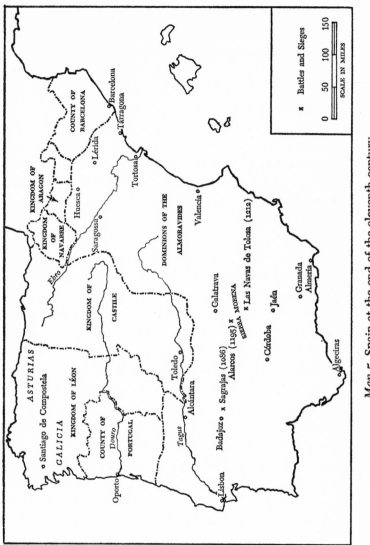

Map 5. Spain at the end of the eleventh century

traditions, customs, and laws as a direct heir of the old Visigothic kingdom. Léon and Castile, which had evolved from the earlier kingdom, were not directly exposed to feudal influence and were only superficially affected by the institutions that had been developed in France north of the Loire. The states which emerged farther to the east, particularly Aragon and Barcelona, were more subject to Frankish influence, and this was reflected in their political and military institutions. Barcelona, or Catalonia, came into existence as the Spanish March, which had been set up during the last quarter of the eighth century in the course of the Frankish expansion under Charlemagne. For many years the March was governed by Frankish counts, and its institutions were framed in imitation of those of the Carolingian empire. Conversely considerable modification of the nascent Frankish feudalism took place as a result of the influence of local traditions.

As the Frankish empire began to fall apart in the middle decades of the ninth century, Carolingian monarchs with neither the energy nor the resources to devote to the defense of such remote territories as the Spanish March left the frontier increasingly vulnerable to attacks by the Moslems. Unlike the underpopulated lands which faced Léon and Castile, the Catalonian frontier overlooked the Ebro Valley, which had populous and well-fortified cities such as Huesca, Saragossa, and Lérida, whose Moslem marcher lords found the ill-defended frontier a tempting invitation they could not afford to decline. The incursion of 851–852 resulted in the capture and sack of Barcelona itself. Left to its own defenses, the Spanish March broke up into a number of counties, acquired new rulers of native stock, and began to work out systems of land tenure and military service which, although they owed something to Frankish institutions, were essentially designed to meet the requirements of protecting and then developing the frontier.

The process by which Frankish counts were replaced by rulers of local origin was not revolutionary, and the new counts recognized the suzerainty of the Carolingians until well into the tenth century. The changeover to local rulers was complete by the late 870's. The problem of land tenure must be dealt with at greater length, not only because of its greater complexity, but because landholding and military service were usually connected. In ninth-century Catalonia most of the land was allodial, as it was in southern France, but there were also beneficial holdings of varying size and importance. There were farmer-vassals who paid rent living beside more important tenants who held their lands of the count in return for military service. Between allodial land and beneficed land was the *aprisio*. This was to be of great importance in Catalan colonizing activity in lands reconquered from the Moors. During the course of the ninth century, benefices, as they did elsewhere in the Frankish realm, became hereditary, and there was an increasing tendency for both *aprisiones* and benefices to become allods, although the holder remained in a state of individual vassalage.

Shortly after Guifred became count of Barcelona, about 880, he began to push southward and southwestward in an attempt to secure a more defensible frontier. He reoccupied the former county of Ausona, in the Plain of Vich, which had been abandoned earlier in the century. Old strongholds were repaired and new ones were constructed, to insure permanent occupation. At the same time Guifred began to push his frontier south in the direction of Tarragona and Lérida. These were modest gains, but they established a pattern which was to be consistently followed by the later counts of Barcelona and kings of Aragon in securing new territory.

The Plain of Vich and other vacant lands were granted as *aprisiones*, not only to members of the baronage, but to ecclesiastical corporations as well. While most of the new land apparently was colonized by nobles and the church, lands were also assigned to freemen of the lesser sort, who, however, owed some dues for them. The major frontier landholders were relieved of certain fiscal burdens in return for an increased obligation to military service. As the land returned to cultivation, the *aprisiones* became allodial property. There is also some evidence to suggest that, at least in the county of Ausona, the castles became centers for organizing the recently occupied land. It is quite obvious that the plan of settlement or colonization was not feudal, since the counts of Barcelona did not grant fiefs to their vassals.

As the century drew to a close, Catalan encroachment had become sufficiently serious to cause alarm among the Moslem rulers of the Ebro Valley. Beginning in 897, the Catalan counties were subjected to a series of devastating raids that lasted for nearly twenty years. The impunity with which Moslem columns penetrated into the very heart of Catalonia and the ease with which Christian armies were defeated in the field indicate that the frontier castles and the traditional levy of all free men were not very effective in protecting the interior from destructive Moorish raids. Unless an enemy is intent on occupying territory, he will pay no attention to the fortresses but simply bypass them, since the garrisons, individually, are powerless to stay his advance. Permanent conquest called for an expenditure of time and resources that were apparently as scarce in Moorish Spain as they were in the Christian states crowded against the Pyrenees. Only in very unusual circumstances were the Christian or Moorish rulers able to make really substantial gains.

During the period from about 914 to 975, when the rulers of the various Catalan counties acknowledged the overlordship of the Ummayad emir of Córdoba, the extension of the frontiers toward the Ebro continued. The advances were closely connected with the construction of new castles which served as centers for the organization of the frontier. There is a similarity between the expansion of the Catalans at the expense of their Moslem neighbors in the tenth century and the extension of the Anglo-Norman frontier into Wales in the latter part of the eleventh century. The palatine earldoms established by King William I were largely independent, and the conquests in Wales were, with few exceptions, due to the initiative of the marcher lords themselves, although the lands they conquered were held by knight service instead of allodially. In Catalonia, as in the Midi, the tenth century also saw the evolution of a new class of warriors on the frontier. Permanent garrisons of *milites* were stationed in the border castles who served full time and drew their support from dues levied on the surrounding lands. It is a temptation to call these *milites* mercenaries, since their service did not depend on landholding; whatever their precise status, it was certainly not feudal.

Despite the increasing militarization of the frontier lands and the construction of castles throughout Catalonia, when warfare was again resumed between Christians and

Moslems about 975, the results were similar to those at the beginning of the century, owing in part to the disintegration of comital authority throughout Catalonia as the magnates, lay and ecclesiastical, sought to increase their power and authority. Thus in 985 the armies of the emir of Córdoba, Al-Mansur (Almansor), were able to capture Barcelona and to devastate Catalonia without fear of retaliation.

Not until the end of the first decade of the eleventh century was there a shift in the balance of power both in the relationship of the counts to their own mightiest subjects and of the Christians to their Moslem neighbors. The revitalization of Catalonia was largely the work of two counts of Barcelona, Ramón Borell (992–1018) and Ramón Berenguer I (1035–1076). In a variety of ways they strengthened the Catalan capacity both to withstand and to launch attacks. Plunder from successful raids was used to buy support from relatives who were established in districts beyond the confines of the county of Barcelona. No attempt was made to disturb the system whereby marcher lords erected strongholds from which to exploit newly conquered lands, but the policy which had enabled them to hold these lands as allods was significantly changed. Not only did the counts take a more active interest in the frontier lands, conducting raids which carried southward as far as the walls of Córdoba, but they also began to compel the marchers to swear fealty in return for continued possession of their castles. The *Reconquista* was made possible by the evolution in Catalonia of a strong central authority able to direct the activities of colonization as well as those of a militant church and a militarized nobility. Unfortunately, it is not possible to say much about the military organization which the counts of Barcelona had at their disposal. While the garrisons of *milites* who occupied the frontier castles are mentioned, it is difficult to find much information about their military capabilities. It may be assumed that the troops whom the counts commanded on raids into Moorish lands were mounted; it is not certain from what sources these troops were raised.

While the Catalans and Aragonese were developing military institutions which were to enable them to compete on equal terms with their Moslem neighbors, the western Spanish kingdoms of Navarre, Léon, and Castile were also expanding southward into the valley of the Douro. Medieval military institutions here owed even less to western feudal practices than did those of Barcelona and Aragon, partly because of the isolated position of the Christians in the mountainous northwest after the remainder of the peninsula had been overrun by the Moslems. Many of the traditions and institutions of the old Visigothic state survived, including an independent nobility and the allodial ownership of property. The spirit of independence was fostered by the nature of warfare on the frontier, which demanded much initiative and enterprise. Moreover, as long as the western kingdoms were confined to the mountainous regions north of the Douro, there was little scope for the employment of cavalry. Hence the traditional infantry levies continued to exercise the dominant role in warfare. Indeed, Sancho Garcia I of Navarre (905–933) was known as Sancho Abarca (the Expediter) because he provided his troops with leather-soled shoes which greatly increased their mobility. The necessity of repopulating the devastated lands recovered from the Moors made the existence of a free, arms-bearing population almost mandatory. In Léon, and to even a greater extent in Castile, the nobles and the free men of the towns exercised an influence that often overshadowed that of the monarchy.

Once the Christian states had pushed their frontiers southward into the plains north of the Douro and the Ebro, of course the necessity for cavalry forces developed. In Léon and Castile this situation occurred as early as the ninth century, in Aragon not until the eleventh. With no powerful aristocracy which had the resources to establish vast estates, resettlement was very largely the work of small freeholders. Since all lordless land belonged to the crown, as the reconquest progressed large tracts became available which kings could grant to lay or ecclesiastical magnates or retain under royal control. Easy terms were offered to attract settlers; in late-eleventh-century Castile, the king or a lord might even give a free man both horse and armor in return for military service. Usually, however, the free settlers seem to have been sufficiently well-off to supply their own mounts and equipment. Moreover, each newly liberated town was divided into *caballerías* (cavalry portions) and *peonías* (infantry portions) which were granted to settlers who would accept the attached military obligations.

The process of encouraging the resettlement of recovered land led to the emergence of one of the most important military classes in medieval Spain—the *caballeros villanos*, nonnoble knights. As early as the struggle between Léon and Castile in the eleventh century there is some mention of these mounted commoners, but their importance steadily increased after the fall of Toledo to Alfonso VI in 1085 and during the period of the subsequent

Almoravide threat. Their number grew as many new towns were founded during the eleventh and twelfth centuries in the new frontier lands between the Douro and the Tagus rivers. Grants to *caballeros villanos* were termed benefices, but these were more in the nature of the *beneficia* of Merovingian times in Gaul than the military benefices instituted by the early Carolingians. Frequently some semiservile labor dues were attached to the grant, and the mounted commoners were at first classified with the taxpaying subjects. Like the conditional benefice of Carolingian times, the grant reverted to the donor on the death of the recipient. However, the need for this category of warrior became so pressing that by the second decade of the twelfth century it was customary to grant hereditary rights to horse and armor, even if the heir was a minor.

By the mid-tenth century, the position of Léon as leader of the western Spaniards was being challenged by the frontier county of Castile. The Léonese kings had found it expedient to entrust the administration of their eastern frontier districts to counts who were actually resident there. This was an arrangement not dissimilar to that found in the border marks of the German kingdom or in the palatine earldoms of Norman England. The magnates would have a personal stake in protecting the frontiers from Moorish raids and in expanding their territories at the expense of the infidel. This plan, if plan it was, worked well during the ninth century. The Christian advance, though fiercely contested, moved relentlessly southward. Fighting raged back and forth across the contested land, and many districts changed hands several times before Spanish occupation became permanent. The frontiersmen, constantly under arms, studded the land with castles to protect themselves against sudden Moorish incursions, thereby giving the name Castile to the whole region. By the beginning of the tenth century, the counts of Castile were beginning to adopt an independent attitude toward their nominal suzerains, the kings of Léon. On occasion they even ignored summons to military duty on the grounds that they could not afford to leave the frontier defenseless. The goal of Castilian independence was achieved by the end of the tenth century, and although many a long and bitter civil struggle took place before the final union of the two kingdoms in the twelfth century, leadership in western Spain passed irrevocably to Castile.

For this reason, Castilian military practices and institutions were characteristic of western Spain throughout the so-called feudal period. The nobles were of especial importance, since their principal occupation was fighting. Their primary duty was to appear at the muster whenever summoned by the king, with whatever forces each could bring into the field. However, this responsibility was a personal one; a noble performed military service because he was a noble, and not because he held land that carried a military obligation. In this respect the Spanish noble more nearly resembled the English thegn than he did the feudal baron. The upper levels of the nobility (*ricos hombres*) were entitled to an invitation rather than a summons to duty, but they were always supposed to accept it. They were also entitled to display a standard and a caldron, emblems of their right and competence to raise and maintain armies at their own expense. The lesser nobility, the hidalgos, had fewer privileges. At the bottom of the scale were the *caballeros*, roughly equivalent to knights or *chevaliers*. Finally, as is noted above, there was an important class of nonnoble knights, the *caballeros villanos*. These had no equivalent in the feudal hierarchy of western Europe and can be compared only to the nonnoble citizens of the Italian communes who owed cavalry service because of their economic position rather than their social status. A considerable number of the knights resided in the towns and doubtless contributed much to the steadiness of the city levies.

Among the nobility, ties of vassalage existed, but they were not very binding. A vassal might renounce his fealty to his lord by making a simple declaration of renunciation; a similar freedom of action was enjoyed by the Aragonese nobility. Vassalage in Spain cannot be called feudal; it bears some resemblance to the status of the old English free man who "could go with his land to whatever lord he would." Another factor that helped prevent the development of the landed benefice was the circulation of money in apparently far greater quantities in Spain than in the feudal society north of the Alps. As early as the tenth century, it is stated, a benefice might be either land or money. In the eleventh century, following the breakup of the Ummayad caliphate of Córdoba, the rulers of the succession states (*taifas*) began to pay heavy annual tribute to the Christian rulers. This resulted in a great increase in cash payment to their vassals—analogous, perhaps, to the money fief in western Europe, but on a much larger scale.

Despite the fragility of the bonds of vassalage, the nobles formed the backbone of the armies with which the kings of Castile fought the long wars of the *Reconquista*. There were, however, other sources of military manpower. The higher clergy were supposed to accompany the king on his campaigns against the Moors, and a kind of scutage was assessed against those who were unable to appear at the muster. Late in the twelfth century the founding of the great military orders of Calatrava (1158), Santiago (*ca.* 1168), and Alcántara (1183) also strengthened the military position of Castile. Their knights did valiant service against the Moors down to the middle of the thirteenth century, but as in Crusader Syria, the orders became so powerful that they constituted a standing menace to the state. The nobles and the knights of the military orders provided the nucleus of heavy cavalry common to most western armies. The surviving carvings and manuscript illuminations of the eleventh century show little difference between the arms and equipment of Spanish knights and those of northern Europe. The steel cap is round instead of conical, and the mail coat appears to have a collar that can be turned up to protect the lower part of the face; these seem to be the only differences.

On the other hand, some Spanish techniques were borrowed from the Moorish foes. For the constant raids that characterized warfare on the frontier, mobility was a factor of the highest importance. The increasingly heavy horse and panoply of the western knight found only limited acceptance on the Iberian Peninsula. Instead, a distinctive style, *á la jinete,* evolved, characterized by short stirrups, a fairly low saddle, a palate bit, and directing the horse by neck-reining.[1] Eventually the riders devel-

---

[1] The Moors and their Christian imitators used palate bits with high ports, and they rode with their hands held high, relying on pressure of the high port against the roof of the palate to stop the horse. They depended on neck-reining to turn their mounts, instead of pressure of the bit on the corners of the mouth and lips, which was the ordinary method north of the Pyrenees, where the knights sat straight-legged in high-cantled saddles with long stirrups.

oped into the celebrated light cavalry (*genitours*), who were admirably suited to the hit-and-run tactics of frontier warfare but completely unable to withstand the charge of heavy cavalry of the western European type.

Another source of manpower was the city levies, frequently referred to in accounts of campaigns against the Moors. While many towns had gained exemption from all military obligations except defending their own walls, some regarded their martial exploits with pride, whether on campaign against the infidel or in settling accounts with a troublesome local baron. The presence of large numbers of *caballeros* in the towns, coupled with the record of raids into Moorish territory, indicates that a large proportion of the municipal contingents were mounted. Indeed, some towns took measures to insure that everyone who was financially able to perform mounted service did so. In some instances the municipal officials had the authority to seize and sell the property of a man who had the means to buy a horse and had failed to do so. From the proceeds of the sale he was furnished a proper mount. As was the case in many Italian cities, the obligation to perform cavalry service depended upon a man's economic position, and not solely upon his social status. If, for any reason, he lost this position, he fell to the ranks of the tax-paying infantry; a twelfth-century Portuguese statute clearly distinguishes between the *miles per naturum* who did not lose his knightly rank if he lost his horse and the *miles non per naturum* who did.[2]

The responsibilities of the arms-bearing population of exposed frontier districts must have been extremely oner-

[2] Elena Lourie, "A Society Organized for War: Medieval Spain," *Past and Present,* No. 35 (Dec. 1966), 72.

ous. Although the *caballeros villanos* had become the most important military element in the towns by the twelfth century, all knights, noble as well as nonnoble, were committed to the defense of their own towns and the surrounding villages. Even in peacetime this involved what would today be called police functions—guarding the range lands and patrolling the frontier. The threat of Moorish raids was constant, and among both Christians and Moslems horse-thievery and cattle-rustling offered lucrative opportunities. Such activities, it might be noted, were by no means directed only at the livestock of members of the opposite faith.

It would appear that the kings of the two principal Spanish kingdoms—Castile and Aragon—had adequate manpower resources from which to recruit their armies. But the lack of unity and discipline was deplorable. There was every likelihood that many contingents would desert at the outset if their commanders disapproved of the plan of campaign or if there was little prospect of plunder. The king would actually consider himself fortunate if none of his troops was found eventually in the ranks of the enemy. Even in the few instances in which the whole army remained loyal to the king, the great number, the lack of uniform size among the contingents, the wide variety in the armament and level of training, and above all the lack of an adequate chain of command made real efficiency impossible. The only reason that the armies of the Spanish kingdoms won their fair share of victories was that Moorish commanders were usually plagued with the same problems.

In spite of the religious factors involved in the *Reconquista*, neither side was at all reluctant to employ mercenaries of the other faith. Christian knights were much in demand by Moslem rulers, and even so redoubtable a warrior as Rodrigo Díaz y Vivar—the celebrated Cid (*ca.* 1043–1099)—did not hesitate to employ Moorish troops or to serve Moslem rulers. Some similarity may be detected to practices in Norman Italy and Sicily, where long contact between Christian and Moslem had also bred mutual respect for the other's military capabilites.

The career of the Cid exemplifies the possibilities open to an able and not overly sensitive free-lance commander. Exiled by the king of Castile for some real or fancied offense, the Cid served successively the emirs of Saragossa and Valencia, then struck out on his own. His personal following (*mesnada*) eventually grew into a private army of several thousand—the chroniclers usually give the figure 7000—which enabled him to conduct operations as a virtually sovereign prince. The Cid was a commander of rare skill, both as a strategist and a tactician, and the only Christian general who was able to defeat the dreaded Almoravides. And he possessed that intangible quality of being able to inspire his own troops while instilling misgivings in those of his enemies.

Perhaps the foregoing paragraphs have drawn too unfavorable a picture of the military scene in medieval Spain. It is certainly true that the means were often inadequate, but the generalship was frequently of a high order and strategic planning was not unknown. Not only was there frequent military cooperation between Castile and Aragon, but treaties in 1151 and 1179 established in outline the future course of the *Reconquista*.

Of considerable interest are the combined operations, such as the abortive attacks on Valencia and Tortosa in

1092 by Alfonso VI of Castile (1065–1109), Sancho Ramírez of Aragon (1063–1094), and Berenguer Ramón II of Barcelona (1082–1096) in cooperation with the fleets of Genoa and Pisa. More successful was the operation against Almería in 1147, which resulted in the capture of the city by the kings of Castile and Aragon and the count of Barcelona, assisted by the Genoese fleet. In the same year Lisbon fell to Count Affonso Henriques of Portugal (1112–1185), aided by a flotilla of English and Flemish Crusaders who interrupted their voyage to the Holy Land in order to help capture this important city. In 1148, the Genoese fleet, which had wintered at Barcelona after the capture of Almería, aided the count in taking the town of Tortosa, although the citadel continued to hold out for more than a year.

For the prosecution of such sieges, the standard engines of medieval Europe were employed—catapults, movable wooden towers, and battering rams. They were no more effective in Spain than elsewhere, and a city usually could be reduced only through treachery or hunger. It was seldom that a Christian king could establish a regular investment; thus a blockade was the only practical method of starving out a town. To protect the blockaders against the attacks of a relieving force, fortified base camps were set up from which operations were directed. In 1091 the king of Aragon constructed such a camp for his blockade of Saragossa, and again while operating against Huesca in 1094. In his blockade of Valencia in 1093 the Cid built a fortified camp at Juballa, to the north of the city.

The capture of Toledo by Alfonso VI in 1085 convinced the rulers of the Moslem emirates that their own resources were inadequate to halt the Christian advance. Some of them, under the leadership of Motamid of Seville, reluctantly sought the aid of Yusuf ibn Teshufin, ruler of the Almoravide empire in North Africa. Yusuf first secured a bridgehead by occupying the port of Algeciras, and on about 30 June 1086, landed with a large army, including Turkish archers who were almost certainly mercenaries. The intervention of the Almoravides completely altered the political and military balance between Christian and Moslem on the peninsula and introduced tactical novelties which Christian commanders had difficulty in learning to counter effectively. Shortly after landing, Yusuf was joined by Moorish contingents from Seville, Granada, and Málaga; later the levies of Badajoz and contingents sent by the emir of Almería augmented Moslem strength.

At the time of the Almoravide landing, Alfonso of Castile was engaged in besieging the Moorish city of Saragossa. He raised the siege and at once began to muster an army for operations against the invaders and their Moorish allies. The composition of this army is not known precisely. In addition to the levies of Castile and Léon, contingents were sent by King Sancho Ramírez of Aragon. The Castilian mercenary force in Valencia under Alvar Hañez was recalled, and individual knights from France and Italy are reported to have joined Alfonso's standard. Since the decisive action was not fought until nearly the end of October, the king had sufficient time to get his army in some sort of shape before taking the field. Probably about the beginning of October, Alfonso marched south to meet the enemy, whom he found camped near Sagrajas, some five miles from Badajoz, on 20 October. The Christian army apparently went into camp about three miles from the Moslems, with the river Guardiana (or Guerrero) separating them. For the next three days the armies sat and watched each other while messengers passed back and forth attempting to set a date for the battle. Doubtless these messengers were also charged with picking up whatever information they could about the size, composition, and disposition of the enemy forces. Nothing can be said with certainty about the size of either army, although the Christian host was probably inferior in numbers. Little more is known about the order of battle employed by each commander. Yusuf placed the camp of his Andalusian allies, in whom he put little confidence, in front of his own, which was defended by a wide ditch, with a hill separating the two camps. The Moorish contingents were probably intended to receive the impact of any Christian advance, to slow it down, and perhaps to throw its ranks into disorder. The main Almoravide line lay to the rear, and Yusuf also seems to have made provisions for a tactical reserve. Of the Christian order of battle, all that can be said is that Alfonso's troops attacked in two divisions, one behind the other, with possibly some provision for a camp guard.

Before daybreak on 23 October (Friday, the Moslem Sabbath), while Motamid was still at morning prayer, his pickets came riding in to report that the Christian army was on the move. Motamid had time to form a line of battle before the leading elements of Alfonso's army crashed into it. These consisted of the Aragonese contingents commanded by the mercenary captain, Alvar Hañez. Soon the Andalusian line fell into almost complete disorder, and most of the units were in full flight in the direction of Badajoz, with Hañez and his troopers pursuing energetically. Only the Sevillians under Motamid managed to hold their ground. During this preliminary encounter Yusuf made no move to bolster his first line.

In the meantime, the Christian main body commanded by King Alfonso came ino action. It hit the Moslem main line, and the more heavily mounted and armed Europeans broke the African front, crossed the ditch, and reached the Almoravide camp. But now Yusuf's superiority in manpower began to make itself felt. The Moslem commander still had uncommitted reserves which he began to feed into the line. The remnant of the Andalusian contingents, still doggedly fighting under Motamid, were reinforced by a division of Moroccan tribesmen directed by Yusuf's most trusted lieutenant, Syr Abu ibn Bekr. With other fresh troops, Yusuf himself apparently swept around the Christian flank and fell upon the rearward elements guarding Alfonso's camp. When the king received news of the attack on his rear, he held a hasty council with his available subordinates, and a decision was made to withdraw from the advanced position, which might well become a trap. A withdrawal under such circumstances frequently becomes a rout, and to the credit of the Spanish knights, it was made in good order despite heavy casualties, and Alfonso successfully established a new line.

It was during this phase of the action that the Christian knights were first exposed to the famous Almoravide drums. The authorities are agreed that the incessant drumbeat was a stratagem designed to encourage the Moslem troops and to demoralize those of the enemy. It is not so certain that the Almoravide units were trained to maneuver on the battlefield in response to orders transmitted by some kind of drum code. In any event, the Spanish troops were confused by the drumming as well as impressed by the compact and disciplined formations of the Almoravides. The Christian knights were accustomed to a melee in which individual skill and courage was the key to victory. They were better armed, better mounted, and probably more skilled in the use of their weapons than their Moslem adversaries, but in mass they were unable to withstand the onslaughts of the steadier African formations.

By the time Alfonso had re-established a line in front of his camp, Hañez had apparently rallied part of the Aragonese horse and had returned to the field. He decided that he did not like the situation and withdrew at once. The retreat of Hañez and his troopers put new heart into the remnants of the Moslem first line, and even Andalusians who had fled toward Badajoz turned back to the battlefield. This enabled Yusuf to concentrate his entire available force on Alfonso and the Christian main body, whose position grew more desperate as the day wore on. Finally, the Almoravide commander threw his last reserve—the Black Guard, said to be 4000 strong—into the fight. These black Africans apparently formed an elite unit that cut its way through to Alfonso's position and severly wounded the king himself. By nightfall the Christians had been driven from their camp. A remnant of the army, still holding together, managed to reach a neighboring hill where, grouped around the wounded king, it prepared to make a last stand. But under cover of darkness, as the victorious Moslems looted and burned the Spanish camp, Alfonso, accompanied by no more than 500 knights, most of whom were wounded, managed to escape.

In view of the magnitude of the disaster at Sagrajas, the consequences were surprisingly few, for the Moslems failed to exploit their victory to any significant extent. Alfonso thought the situation critical enough to appeal widely throughout Europe for help, darkly hinting that if it were not forthcoming, he would have no choice but to grant the Almoravides the right of free passage through his lands to attack France. The result was an international expedition in 1087 which accomplished practically nothing. On the Moslem side the victory brought a certain enforced unity to Islamic Spain, but that is about all. Yusuf returned almost immediately to Morocco, taking most of his army with him. Only 3000 cavalry were left in Spain under the command of Motamid of Seville, and the Christians had an opportunity to recover from the effects of the shattering defeat.

Without much data about the size or composition of the armies, with no information about the ratio of horse to foot, without anything like an order of battle for either side, it is almost impossible to make any relevant observations about the conduct of the action. It can be guessed that the really decisive factor was Yusuf's preponderance in manpower. Certainly Alvar Hañez' undisciplined pursuit of the Moorish contingents made Alfonso's task more difficult, but it probably only contributed to the magnitude of the Christian defeat. It is difficult to quarrel with Alfonso's decision to pull back his main body from its advanced position, although such a maneuver under combat conditions is always a perilous expedient. Alfonso knew, when he got word of the Almoravide attack on his camp, that he was in imminent danger of being encircled, and he took the only course that offered any hope of escape, that of attempting to regain the camp and to hold out there until nightfall. And the only valid conclusion seems to be that, given his apparent numerical inferiority, Alfonso's principal mistake was in committing himself to a general action in the first place.

The decisive engagement in the long history of the *Reconquista* occurred on 16 July 1212. In 1149 the peninsula had been invaded by a second fanatical Moslem sect from Africa, the Almohades. By 1157 nearly half the peninsula recognized their authority, and in a series of minor campaigns the Christian frontiers had been pushed back to the north. Finally, on 19 July 1195, the Almohades had inflicted a crushing defeat on Alfonso VIII of Castile (1158–1214) at Alarcos, in south-central Spain. As a result, most of the Christians for a time put aside their constant bickering and united against the common enemy. Early in the thirteenth century renewed Christian aggression alarmed the Moors, and Mohammed I of Granada, son of the victor at Alarcos, began to concentrate all available forces for a decisive campaign. Marching northward, he crossed the Sierra Morena and established outposts in the Guadiana Valley. In the meantime, Alfonso VIII sent appeals for help to all his fellow monarchs in Spain, as well as to the pope. Innocent III proclaimed a crusade, and contingents from southern France and other lands north of the Pyrenees joined the great expedition. While it certainly did not have the 60,000 or 100,000 men or the 10,000 horse and 100,000 foot alleged by the chroniclers, it was without doubt the greatest Christian army ever mustered in medieval Spain. In addition to the crusaders, Alfonso commanded the forces of Sancho VIII of Navarre (1194–1234), Pedro II of Aragon (1196–1213), Affonso II of Portugal (1211–1223), and the knights of the military orders, as well as his own Castilians. These kings so far abandoned normal protocol as to serve in person under Alfonso, and only the jealous king of Léon held aloof. After innumerable delays the army, which had concentrated at Toledo, began its southward march on 20 June 1212. Almost at once the heat and hardship of a summer campaign in Spain began to take their toll, and there were large-scale desertions, particularly among the crusaders from north of the Pyrenees. The great majority of the Spanish contingents, however, held together under the leadership of Alfonso.

At the approach of the Christian army, Mohammed withdrew his outposts in the Guadiana Valley, fell back south of the Sierra Morena, and took up a position north of Jaén. By this maneuver he shortened the line of communications to his base at Granada and compelled his enemies to extend theirs through the rugged terrain of the Sierra Morena. The advancing Spaniards found the mountain passes too strongly held to be forced, but a local shepherd guided them through an open defile, and on 13 July the Christian army appeared before the Moslems on the small plain of Tolosa. Here Alfonso went into camp, and for the next two days the antagonists faced each other, with neither making a move. It may be supposed that Mohammed used the opportunity to strengthen his position, for the Moslem center, where the Moorish commander established his command post, was fortified by a palisade bound together with heavy chains.

There is no way of estimating the size of the two armies on the eve of the engagement. The Cid, late in the eleventh century, is reputed to have commanded as many as 7000 men; in 1089, Alfonso VI of Castile concentrated 18,000 men at Toledo for a campaign against the Moors—

a high but not impossible figure. In 1214, Philip II of France was able to put about 27,000 men into the field. The campaign of 1212 approached a national effort, with four of the five reigning Christian monarchs participating in person. It may be supposed, therefore, that national prestige was at stake and that extraordinary means were taken to put troops into the field. As a guess, then, it seems possible that Alfonso had as many as 25,000 to 30,000 effectives to put into the line when he decided to take the offensive on the morning of 16 July.

The Castilian king had organized his army into the three divisions common to medieval orders of battle. The center was made up of the Castilian contingents under the personal command of Alfonso. The left wing, commanded by King Pedro of Aragon, also included the contingents of Archbishop Rodrigo of Toledo and those of the Knights of Santiago and of Calatrava. King Sancho of Navarre commanded the right wing. The action was unique, for each division of the army fought under a reigning monarch. Alfonso does not seem to have provided for a tactical reserve, although the infantry levies may have acted in such a capacity. The Almohade order of battle cannot be reconstructed, and the statement that Mohammed had 100,000 cavalry in line with strong infantry support may be dismissed out of hand.

The engagement opened with a Spanish charge all along the line, and violent fighting raged back and forth across the plain. Slowly the heavier horses and arms of the Christian knights began to gain ground. In the center, however, the Moslems offered a sturdy resistance. It seems that late in the day Mohammed delivered a counterstroke with his center that would have been successful if the Spanish infantry levies had not beaten off the charges of the Moorish horse and given the knights a chance to reform. During this interval the Christian right wing of Sancho of Navarre apparently rolled up the Moslem left and reached Mohammed's stockaded command post. The Moorish leader then conceded victory and with his bodyguard fled toward Baeza, leaving his army to be annihilated where it stood as the whole Spanish line swept forward.

Although Moorish losses were certainly fewer than the 125,000 to 150,000 reported by contemporary Christian chroniclers, they must have been substantial, and the fate of the Moslems in Spain was sealed. In the short run, however, the victory failed to produce immediate results. Alfonso was unable to hold his army together long enough to exploit his success, and the immediate danger was no sooner eliminated than the erstwhile allies were fighting among themselves as bitterly as ever.

Warfare in southern France and Christian Spain during the early Middle Ages provides little novelty. Surprisingly, though these societies were "feudal" in only the most superficial way, their responses to the military demands of the times differed from those of more completely feudalized states only in the manner in which troops were raised. The military tenure of northern France found little acceptance south of the Loire before the end of the eleventh century, and south of the Pyrenees none at all. Military service was the obligation of every free man, and was not determined by any land that he might hold. On the other hand, the castle, long considered to be the very symbol of feudal society was as much a part of the medieval landscape of the Midi and Christian Spain as it was of the Ile de France or Norman England. The knights who entered Toledo with Alfonso VI of Castile in 1085 or who fought beneath the standards of Calatrava and Santiago a century later differed in no significant respects from those who served under Guiscard at Civitate in 1053 or who followed the banners of the Hospital and the Temple in Crusader Syria. Spanish as well as Lombard and German commanders were aware of the value of good infantry, and they learned how to use it to advantage on the battlefield. The nonfeudal troops of Count Raymond Saint-Gilles of Toulouse do not seem to have been less effective on the First Crusade than the feudal contingents of Robert of Normandy or Bohemund of Taranto. The tactics of Sagrajas and Las Navas de Tolosa differed little from those of Nocera or Hastings. It can only be concluded that though military institutions—the methods of raising armies—differed widely between the France of the early Capetians and contemporary states south of the Loire and beyond the Pyrenees, these institutions had very little effect on what commanders did with the soldiers once they were mustered and committed to operations.

7

Town versus Country: Feudal Wars in Central and Northern Italy

When Charlemagne assumed the Iron Crown of Lombardy in 774, the introduction of Frankish institutions into the transalpine conquests was inevitable. Although in the abstract the former Lombard kingdom was ruled as a separate state, the *capitularia* (decrees) of the great Charles ran throughout all the lands which were subject to his control. At first glance it might seem that Lombard Italy would be particularly receptive to Frankish customs. Among the Germanic peoples, the latest to settle on former imperial soil were the Lombards, who, at the time of their conquest by the Franks, were scarcely more than two centuries away from a barbaric and nomadic condition. In those centuries, although the Lombards had acquired a material culture which was probably superior to that of the Franks, their military institutions, owing to the political patterns developed in the peninsula, had not become as specialized as those of the Frankish state. In some ways the military organization of the Lombards resembled that of the Franks before the introduction of the military benefice.

The Lombard term for free man was *arimannus* (army man) or *exercitalis*, reflecting the obligation of every free male to perform military service in time of war. As in the other Germanic kingdoms, the individual warrior was expected to provide his own equipment. It is interesting that Lombard military legislation suggests a higher level of economic development in Italy than that in the contemporary kingdom of the Franks. Lombard law, suggestive of the much later Assize of Arms (1181) of Henry II in England, divided the free population into three economic classes for determining the equipment with which each individual should be armed. The wealthiest landowners—those who possessed seven or more manses of land—were expected to appear at the muster with mail shirt (lorica), shield, lance, and horse. The second category—those who held less than seven manses but at least forty jugera (a land measure of unknown extent)—were required to have shield, lance, and horse. All other free men had to appear with shield, bow, and arrows. It is of great significance that the merchant population was sufficiently numerous and wealthy to be classified for military service along with the landholders. Also of significance is the fact that two of the three classes of free men were required to come mounted to the host. Unfortunately, the sources are not clear as to whether these horsemen fought as cavalry or merely used horses on the march. Although the largest number of free men must have belonged to the third class and served as infantry, there is evidence to suggest that at least some military engagements were fought by mounted troops.

In time of war each free man was expected to follow his duke or royal *gastaldius*, but it seems highly unlikely that the whole levy of the Lombard kingdom was called out frequently. When a major offensive campaign was undertaken against the Byzantines or when a Frankish invasion threatened, undoubtedly the general levy was summoned to duty. But, as is noted above in connection with pre-Conquest England, most campaigns were on a smaller scale and more localized, requiring the levies of a more restricted area. So, in general, the individual Lombard warrior would probably perform most of his military service close to home under the command of local officials. The local duke or *gastaldius* would call out the levy of his territory to repel Moslem or Byzantine raids. On numerous occasions the men of Friuli were summoned by their duke to protect this exposed northeastern frontier from incursions by the Avars and other peoples of the middle Danube. To the south, the dukes of Spoleto and Benevento frequently called out their men with or without royal authorization. Far from the seat of royal authority, these dukes were virtually independent and pursued their own policies; their military forces were as frequently employed in aggressive action against the Byzantines of lower Italy as in defending the frontiers of their realms. But in spite of serving frequently under local commanders in largely local campaigns, it seems certain that until the late seventh and early eighth centuries, the Lombard warrior, because of his position as a free man, regarded military service as an obligation to the entire people.

By the late seventh century, however, a new development was evident which eventually made the military service of the free man, especially of the poorer sort, less important. This was a revival of the old Germanic practice of recruiting a band of personal followers not unlike the primitive comitatus or the *fideles* of Merovingian and early Carolingian times. Sworn followers (*gasindii*) appear more frequently in Lombard sources in the course of the eighth century. Just as the great magnates of Merovingian Gaul with their bands of sworn dependents had undermined royal authority, so the Lombard dukes—there were as many as thirty-five such dignitaries—with their *gasindii* reduced the effectiveness of royal power in the Lombard kingdom and threatened royal control over the armed forces. Lords intervened to protect their followers, who, in turn, pledged their allegiance to their lord rather than the king. The tendency toward hereditary succession and independence in Lombard duchies had always been a factor with which the kings had to contend. By the middle of the eighth century this trend toward disintegration had been greatly accelerated by the growth of the practice of personal commendation, similar to vassalage, and the resulting weakening of royal military power, since the *gasindii* were among the best trained and best equipped members of the army. This practice contributed in no small measure to the ineffective resistance to the Frankish invasions of 755 and 774.

The Carolingian conquest was certain to have a significant impact on the military institutions of Lombard Italy. Although the kingdom retained its identity and was not incorporated into the Frankish state, from the start Franks were substituted for Lombards in high offices. The Lombard dukes were not summarily removed, but as duchies became vacant or were confiscated on some pretext, they were usually bestowed on a loyal Frank, together with the title of count. Only in Spoleto and Benevento, where Frankish authority was at best nominal, did native dynasts continue to rule until the Norman conquest of the eleventh century. Carolingian policy with respect to the Lombard duchies is similar to that followed three hundred years later by William the Conqueror in dealing with the English earldoms. To insure royal control of the administrative machinery, the system of *missi dominici* was extended to Italy. The decentralizing trends so evident in the last years of Lombard rule were halted, although in general Lombard organization was retained and local laws and customs were respected. Nor was any change made in the Lombard custom of exacting military service from all free men. The almost annual campaigns of Charlemagne imposed a considerable strain on Frankish manpower, which must have been measurably relieved when he was able to add Lombard resources to his own. The military legislation of Charlemagne, discussed in an earlier chapter, was also extended to the Lombard kingdom, but the granting of land on beneficial tenure in return for mounted military service appeared only gradually.

As has been already noted, vassalage, in the form of the lord-*gasindiis* relationship, had become steadily more important in the Lombard state in the course of the eighth century. But there is no evidence to show that this personal bond was in any way associated with landholding. Even after the Frankish conquest, grants of land, though they were to individuals often described as *vassi* or *fideles*, were given as rewards for past services, and only much later did the military benefice become of real significance. Even when it did, although powerful benefice holders were soon able to make their lands hereditary, it was not until the eleventh century, and after a long and bitter struggle, that undertenants were able to pass on their benefices to their heirs. Titles not only became hereditary but divisible among heirs, and by the beginning of the tenth century any man with any sort of pretensions was a marquis, or a count at the very least. The imperfect and irregular development of feudalism in Italy was one of the factors which favored the growth of urban independence.

The strong hand of Charlemagne was able to hold the disruptive tendencies of feudalism in check both north of the Alps and in Italy. The recruitment of private armies was forbidden; counts and ecclesiastical tenants were required to answer military summons in person and with all their vassals. But when the Frankish dominions fell to weaker hands, the decentralizing process resumed with increasing acceleration. The absence of any real law of succession, the Frankish custom of dividing the state among all surviving sons, and renewed attacks on Europe by external enemies all combined to reduce the Frankish empire to a shambles, with each section thereafter going its own way and developing its own political and military institutions to fit its own needs.

Nowhere was the confusion more absolute than in Italy. The end of the Carolingians in Italy, which came in 888, was followed by near anarchy which lasted until the intervention of the German king, Otto, three-quarters of a century later. Incredibly complex struggles between contenders for the empty title of king—mostly of Burgundian or Lombard origin and claiming to be descended from Charlemagne—were coupled with the savage attacks of Moslems and Magyars. The result was that the political and military structure of Italy collapsed completely. It is necessary to describe what happened to the pieces if Italian feudal warfare is to be understood at all.

One of the elements of Carolingian military administration was the border county or march. These were established on the more exposed frontiers of the empire, and their administrative heads (*Markgrafen,* marquis) were entrusted with greater authority than ordinary counts, as has been noted earlier. The combination of civil and military authority—was it borrowed from the Byzantine strategos?—enabled the *Markgraf* to mobilize the resources of his county more rapidly and more effectively in times of military crisis.

The idea of special frontier districts was not unknown to the Lombards. Very soon after the Lombard occupation of northern Italy, the frontier duchy of Friuli had been established. This covered the gap in Italy's mountain defenses through which the Lombards themselves had entered the peninsula; the duchy of Friuli was created to prevent further Germanic invasions and to halt incursions by the Avars and Slavs who milled about in the Danube basin. Friuli also served as a check against the northward expansion of the Byzantine exarchate of Ravenna. The duchy of Spoleto had been a true frontier district in origin, wedged between the exarchate and the nominally Byzantine duchy of Rome. Its distance from the royal seat of power at Pavia, however, made the duke of Spoleto a virtually independent potentate who often defied the authority of the king. The duchy of Benevento, even farther to the south, was not so much a frontier district as an enclave, virtually surrounded by Byzantine territory.

The first of the Carolingian marches in Italy was the

duchy, or march, of Friuli. The military considerations which had led the Lombards to put special emphasis on the exposed northeastern frontier persuaded the Franks to do the same. Somewhat later a count of Lucca got himself recognized as *Markgraf* of the mountainous region of central Italy eventually known as the march of Tuscany. And although the old Lombard duchy of Spoleto never gave more than nominal obedience to the Frankish rulers of Italy, it became to all intents and purposes a march when its rulers were granted, or assumed, the title of marquis before the end of the ninth century.

Each of these areas had a military *raison d'être* in the eighth and ninth centuries. Friuli was a shield against the Avars in the late eighth century, although a hundred years later it afforded but scant protection against the inroads of the Magyars. The Tuscan march faced the Moslems in Sardinia and to a degree acted as a check on those who had established a base at Frassineto, on the Riviera. Later the march of Ivrea was created to protect the passes from France into Italy from incursions by the Riviera Moslems. Spoleto, of course, faced the Byzantine theme of Langobardia and the Moslems who operated from a strongly fortified base on the river Garigliano. The creation of a march was, however, no guarantee of the security of a frontier. Especially after the death of Charlemagne and the sudden administrative collapse, the great magnates sought only to improve their own positions. The rivals for the crown of Italy in the ninth and tenth centuries attempted to buy the support of powerful nobles by grants of immunity which, in some instances, included immunity from military service. No wonder that military defenses collapsed and that Magyars and Moslems raided almost at will throughout the peninsula.

The petty dynasts who struggled for the empty title of king during the tenth century were utterly unable to protect their subjects from the Hungarians. On those few occasions when the feudal levy took the field against Magyar raiding columns, the results, as is noted later, were disastrous and could not have raised the nobles in the esteem of the townsmen. Their only recourse was the construction of fortifications on a large scale, a development that can clearly be traced throughout the century. Italy, of course, had possessed fortified cities since the time of the Roman Empire, but the surviving evidence suggests that during the late ninth and early tenth centuries, rulers granted laymen and ecclesiastics rights not only to strengthen the walls and towers of towns, but also to construct castles and strong places in the villages and the open countryside. Royal permission seems to have been required for the erection of either public or private fortifications, but in view of the weakness of contemporary kings this was doubtless a formality, and during the century towns, ecclesiastical communities, and nobles were busy surrounding themselves with walls. It may be noted in passing that a community behind its walls was not only more secure against marauding Moslems and Magyars, but it was also in a position to deal more effectively with the local feudal classes. The charters which grant rights to fortify usually specify at some length the structural details which might be incorporated in a given wall or castle. From these details it is fairly clear that the science of fortification in Italy was far more advanced than it was north of the Alps at that time. It seems likely that Roman technical skills had never died out; the towers, wall platforms, and archery apertures described in tenth-century charters contrast sharply with the crude earth and timber structures of the Franks. It may be suspected that the origins of the private, as opposed to the public or civic, fortification should be sought in Italy rather than northern France.

Although the feudal castles of northern and central Italy were to play a significant role in the warfare of the region, the persistence and early revival of urban life, especially in the Po Valley, profoundly influenced the development of military institutions and the course of military history. Italy was almost the only place in western Europe where the older traditions were kept alive, even if in attenuated form. Although scholars have long since given up their attempts to trace the civic institutions of medieval Italian cities to Roman sources, it is certainly true that there did survive some notion of municipal pride and independence. By the time of the Lombard invasions in the late sixth century, citizens of the towns were already beginning to rely on their own efforts for defense. Pavia surrendered to the Lombards in 572 only after a three-year siege—or more likely, blockade. The citizens of Vicenza are said to have participated in a struggle between two Lombard princes shortly before 700.

In the eighth and ninth centuries, the city militias of Rome and Ravenna seem to have been organized on a permanent basis. Already a beginning had been made in the differentiation of the free population into those who bore arms and those who did not. The wealthier elements were known as *optimates militiae;* the middle classes were the *milites.* The former gradually evolved into the great landholding nobles, while the *milites* became the knights and gentry who held fiefs in return for military service. The great allodial proprietors, and the tenants-in-chief of kings, archbishops, and bishops became known as *capitani,* or *cattani.* The inclusion of the great ecclesiastics among the feudal classes followed a pattern observable elsewhere during these disordered times. As their temporal authority increased, archbishops and bishops found it necessary to have military forces at their command and thus were compelled to grant fiefs on military tenure. Although the circumstances are obscure, further evolution took place, and by the tenth century all urban freemen were classified either as *milites* or *cives,* and all seem to have been required to perform military service. In the eleventh century a division among the *milites* developed. The second class of the *milites,* known as *valvassores,* were undertenants of the *capitani.* In the eleventh and twelfth centuries the chief distinction of this civic nobility was that its members fought on horseback, while the great mass of free men performed their military duty on foot. Unlike the feudal classes elsewhere, the nobility of the Italian towns did not form a closed caste; until the late twelfth century it was constantly being augmented from below as commercial and mercantile families were absorbed into it.

In the rural areas, conditions more nearly approached those which obtained in much of feudal Europe. This was especially true in the hill country of the Piedmont and of the rugged terrain of Tuscany, Umbria, and the Romagna. The more powerful of the feudal nobles—descendants of the Lombard *gastaldii* and Carolingian counts—secure in their castles, engaged in the turbulent activities of their contemporaries elsewhere. They fought among themselves and regarded the merchants of the towns with contempt and as legitimate objects for plunder. It was inevitable that conflict should arise between these nobles and the towns, and while little is known of the numerous campaigns that were conducted, slowly but surely most of the neighboring feudal tenants were brought into subjection to the urban authorities. The process was most easily accomplished in Lombardy, where the flat terrain of the Po Valley did not lend itself to the construction of feudal strongholds. By the middle of the twelfth century only the marquis of Montferrat had managed to retain his independence, but even he felt it wise to acquire the status of a citizen of Vercelli before the century was out. In the Piedmont the backwardness of the towns and the rising power of the counts of Savoy favored the retention of feudal authority. It would be a mistake, however, to think of central and northern Italy as completely dominated by the communes. Large areas, particularly in the Romagna and the Alpine foothills, remained under the control of feudal lords and were never subjected by the cities.

It must not be supposed that the reduction of the nobles of the *contado* (countryside) to the authority of the communes or even the requirement—imposed by many cities —that the nobles reside for most of the year within the town walls produced a regime of law and order. The lords, unfortunately, brought their habits to town with them. They built tower houses, such as those that may still be seen in Bologna and that even today dominate the sky line of San Gimignano. They kept large numbers of armed retainers and pursued the bitter private feuds that had characterized their ordinary life in the country. The towns were constantly in tumult as the nobles conducted regular military operations against their local enemies. Attempts were made to limit the height of the towers and to control the fighting from them—as early as about 1100 in Pisa. Similar attempts were made during the twelfth century in Genoa and Bologna, apparently with scant success. Nevertheless, the nobles were an important component of the military forces of the communes. They, as well as the more prosperous citizens, were compelled to maintain horses suitable for cavalry service. Such requirements originated in the early stages of communal development. Ordinarily, an obligated citizen was required to serve in person, although under some circumstances, such as old age, ill health, or infancy, he might be allowed to furnish a substitute. When an estate was divided, the military obligation fell on the joint heirs, a practice which must have complicated the business of organizing the civic levies.

Since the burden of mounted service fell on all those who—according to the tax rolls—could afford it, there were in every commune a fairly large number of men who incurred the obligation although they were not nobles. Such men were known as "knights for the commune" (*milites pro commune*). In some respects this institution was similar to that in many Spanish cities where every man of sufficient means was required to own a horse and to perform cavalry duty. Except in the direst emergency, not all the cavalry were called to duty at any one time. Depending on the military situation, Florence, for example, called out from one to five of its six regions (*sesti*). The citizen who provided a war horse was paid by the commune for its maintenance, and he received compensation if it was injured or killed while in the service of the commune. The citizen himself received pay while on active duty. Indeed, although the first evidence dates only from 1240, it is probable that the Florentine civic levy was paid from the beginning. By 1184, a body of allied Lucchese serving with the Florentines was receiving three *solidi* per day for cavalrymen and one for infantrymen. In 1131 the town of Nonantola agreed to pay the Bolognese militia when it marched to its aid. Such practices did not develop north of the Alps until the thirteenth century was well advanced.

On the less well-to-do free population fell the burden of infantry service. Usually included were all able-bodied males between the ages of fourteen and seventy—although some communes narrowed the eligibility to the eighteen to sixty range. The organization was on a regional basis. The citizen-soldier received some pay while on active duty; the regional officers were entitled to a small stipend throughout the year.

The surrounding countryside (*contado*) controlled by the commune also had its military obligations. Some nobles and dependent communes were responsible for providing fixed numbers of mounted soldiers, but it was customary to divide the rural areas into districts for organizing infantry contingents. At Siena, these districts apparently mustered separately, but in most cities, each quarter had a region of the *contado* attached to it for military purposes. These rural levies were often used for pioneer and engineer service.

By the end of the twelfth century, at least in the larger communes, a considerable amount of administrative apparatus had been developed to handle military matters. By as early as 1162, Pisa had an officer in charge of maintaining the fabric of the walls (*capitanei murorum*). He was responsible for enforcing the compulsory labor of the inhabitants in the construction and maintenance of the fortifications. In some cities each quarter was obliged to provide the labor for its own sector of the walls and its gateway. Officials also had to make decisions—never very popular—as to which individuals would be required to serve mounted; horses had to be inspected, reviewed, and valued. Fines had to be levied and collected in the frequent cases of absence and desertion. When the communal forces were supplemented by mercenaries, these had to be recruited; satisfactory terms had to be negotiated and their observance secured. The paid professional soldier put in an appearance rather later in central and northern Italy than elsewhere. Until the middle of the thirteenth century there were no organized bands that could be hired through their commanders; the soldiers seem to have been hired individually by the communal authorities. While many mercenaries were enrolled in the service of Pope Gregory VII (1073–1085), not until 1124 is there mention of such troops in the pay of a town. In that year Fiesole hired mercenaries in a vain attempt to preserve its independence against neighboring Florence.

Tuscany was the sole Carolingian march to retain its identity much after the end of the tenth century. Here, until the death of the redoubtable Countess Matilda in 1115, the authority of the marquis was unchallenged, and all the resources of Tuscany were at the disposal of its ruler. It was this authority that enabled the countesses Beatrice and Matilda to lend substantial support to the reform papacy of the Hildebrandine era and to defy, with eventual success, the imperial pretensions of both Henry IV and Henry V. Once the strong hand of Matilda was removed, however, Tuscany relapsed into what is often described as feudal anarchy. Where every castle and village was built upon some virtually inaccessible crag, it was easy enough for the great vassals to divide up the lands of the marquisate. In Umbria and the Romagna, feudal families held large contiguous fiefs of the pope, who was often unable to exercise much authority over vassals who from their mountain fastnesses defied both his temporal and spiritual authority. In these regions the struggle between the nobles and the cities was far more protracted and bitter than it was in Lombardy. In the valley of the Arno, the countryside almost to the walls of Florence was dominated by the castles of the nobles, and the early history of the medieval city constitutes a record of constant warfare with its feudal neighbors. This sort of warfare chiefly involved the siege of castles and numerous small-scale combats about which few details remain.

Unfortunately, also, little is known about the number, composition, and organization of the military forces of either the feudal tenants or their urban enemies. It is quite possible that the Countess Beatrice of Tuscany could provide an escort of 500 knights for Pope Nicholas II in 1058, but it is extremely unlikely that Lucca in the twelfth century could put 500 knights and 20,000 infantry into the field, in addition to 5000 horse supplied by the nobles of the *contado*. The total population of Lucca as recently as the beginning of the twentieth century was scarcely 40,000, and it is improbable that the medieval city was as large. More credible is the statement that Milan, the greatest city of Italy, was due the service of 2000 knights, and there are some reasonable figures for the second half of the twelfth century, but certainly the city could not field an army of 50,000. Expect for Milan, the figures would be in hundreds, rather than thousands, for the mounted strength of the northern Italian cities.

The absence of reliable figures makes it almost impossible to generalize about the size of armies, and even less is known about the organization of these forces. In the second quarter of the eleventh century, all the citizens of Milan were assigned to units and armed by Archbishop Aribert, but the nature of the organization is not specified. It may be assumed, however, that he divided the city into wards, or quarters, and that the individual served in the unit from his quarter of the city. Eventually there were six such quarters in Milan, and similar systems are found in many medieval urban centers, including London.

Aribert also established a custom which provided an inspiration and a rallying point for the army in battle. An ox-drawn cart (*carroccio*) was fitted with a staff from which floated the great standard of St. Ambrose. A special guard was posted about the *carroccio*, and its loss in action was considered a civic disgrace. This practice was widely copied by other Italian cities and appeared in England at the battle of the Standard (1138).

Little can be said of the command structure of the city levies. By the beginning of the twelfth century, in many towns the command of the military forces in wartime was entrusted to elected officials known as consuls, whose number varied from place to place and often from year to year. Usually included were representatives of the *capitani*, the *valvassores*, and other free citizens. Such an arrangement obviously violated seriously the principle of unity of command; in 1175 a detachment of 225 Pisan knights marched under two consuls. Nor was it likely to prove a flexible system, and it seems likely that, as with the Roman Republic and the later Swiss Confederation, the command would be in experienced but cautious and mediocre hands. These factors may explain the inability of the Lombard League to undertake major offensive operations or to make wide and permanent conquests. The surprisingly large number of communities that could pursue an independent diplomatic and military policy made cooperation difficult, and coordination, except under exceptional circumstances, all but impossible.

The Franks never settled in Italy in large numbers. Although administrative and military officials were Frankish, the armies they commanded were Lombard. The campaign of 796, in which Charlemagne's son Pepin and Margrave Eric of Friuli decisively defeated the Avars, was fought by a Lombard army. Because the narrative sources for the ninth and tenth centuries are not very satisfactory for reconstructing military events, even such a significant event as the destruction of Avar power is so imperfectly chronicled that authorities are not certain of the exact chronology of the campaigns or who was responsible for the decisive stroke.

One of the better historians of the tenth century was Bishop Luitprand of Cremona, perhaps the best educated man of his day. His description of a campaign will serve to illustrate the difficulties faced by students who attempt to make sense out of ecclesiastical rhetoric.[1] In 898 the Magyars had made what would today be called a reconnais-

[1] *The Works of Luitprand of Cremona*, trans. F. A. Wright (London, 1930), pp. 74–78; C. W. Previte-Orton, "Italy in the Tenth Century," in *Cambridge Medieval History* (New York, 1936), III, 148.

sance in force which penetrated to the river Brenta in the
northeastern corner of Italy. From this advanced post,
scouting parties ranged far and wide. Since the Hungarians were mounted, and since Luitprand says that three
days were devoted to this activity, it may be guessed
that the scouts pushed as far west as Cremona and certainly as far south as the Po. The intelligence reports convinced the commanders of the force that no successful operations could be undertaken with the troops available. The
Magyars therefore withdrew, and during the winter of
898–899 plans were laid for a full-scale attack on Italy
when the weather became more favorable. Thus in the
spring of 899, a major offensive was launched across the
northeastern frontier which, according to Luitprand, carried all the way to Pavia. The king, Berenger I (887–924),
called out the feudal levy, which one authority states numbered 15,000 knights. Luitprand says it was three times
as large as the Hungarian force; elsewhere he claims that
the invaders were too many to be counted. These statements are, of course, irreconcilable, and while it is certainly possible that the Italians outnumbered the Magyars,
that it was anything like 3 to 1 superiority is highly improbable.

The good bishop goes on to relate that the Hungarians,
terrified by the mighty host mustered by King Berenger,
began to flee eastward with the Italians in hot pursuit. At
the crossing of the Adda, nearly thirty miles east of Pavia,
many of the invaders were drowned. The Hungarians then
resorted to negotiations, offering to surrender all their
plunder in exchange for a safe return home. This offer was
rejected by the Italians, who thought that the enemy was
already as good as beaten, so the chase was on again. In

the vicinity of Verona, some sixty miles east of the Adda, a fight took place between the Hungarian rear guard and the Italian advance guard in which—and this is significant —the invaders were having the best of it until the approach of the royal main body caused them to break off the action. The flight continued, on across the Adige and for another thirty-five miles, until the fleeing Magyars reached and crossed the Brenta. By now both men and beasts were in a state of utter exhaustion. Luitprand says nothing about the condition of the pursuers who camped on the west bank of the river, already contemplating the complete destruction of the enemy.

Again the Hungarians offered, in return for safe conduct home, to surrender prisoners, booty, everything save a single horse for each man, and to give hostages as a pledge that never again would they invade Italy. Again the offer was scornfully rejected. On 24 September the Magyars, now desperate, decided that death in battle was preferable to continued flight and probable capture. Setting up, says Luitprand, a triple ambush, the Magyars swarmed across the river straight at the center of the Italian line. The attack was perfectly timed, for apparently many of the king's soldiers had dismounted and were having lunch in camp. Resistance was sporadic; the worthy bishop darkly hints at slackness and even treachery on the part of some of Berenger's troops. Soon the Italians broke and fled, with the Magyars, apparently still on their exhausted horses, at their very heels, butchering the fugitives.

Now, where in all this does the truth lie? First, there is the matter of chronology. It is impossible even to guess the time sequence for the intervening six months between the time the Hungarians launched their invasion in March and the decisive action on 24 September. When did the invaders arrive before Pavia? When did the king issue his military summons? How long did it take the army to assemble? Where did it muster? When did the Magyars decide to retreat? Where were they when this decision was made? If it can be assumed that they were still in the vicinity of Pavia, the chase covered about 130 miles to the Brenta, and the retreat might conceivably have started as late as 17 or 18 September, depending on how much time was consumed by the two parleys. Actually, through Luitprand's turgid rhetoric there can be detected a strategy that was typical of the Magyars and the other nomadic peoples who invaded Europe and the Near East during the Middle Ages. To lure an enemy far from his base by a retreat, to wear him out in the process, to gain time for rest by fruitless negotiations, to lure the foe into a false sense of confidence, and then to attack at a time and place of their own choosing—these were the strategems which led to the defeat of Berenger on the Brenta and which European commanders would not learn to counter effectively for another half century.

Of eleventh-century campaigns, the most interesting is the one waged by Emperor Henry IV against his rebellious vassal, the Countess Matilda of Tuscany, from 1090 to 1092. In the former year the emperor crossed the Alps over the Brenner Pass, determined to crush Pope Urban II and his chief Italian supporter, the indomitable countess. The campaign began with the siege and capture of Mantua by the imperial army. This was an important success, for the fall of Mantua and the defeat of the Tuscan levies at Tricontai opened the way into the heart of Tuscany. Henry then marched south across the Po. One by one Matilda's castles fell into the emperor's hands. By June 1092, Henry was on the heights dominating Modena, and the countess, with the remnants of her army, stood at bay in the hills behind Reggio. At the urging of some of her supporters, she accepted a truce to permit negotiations, but since Matilda would not abandon Urban II and recognize Henry's tame pope, Clement III, hostilities were resumed. In October, the countess was still in the vicinity of Reggio, with strong garrisons in the castles of Bianello and Canossa. Henry then feinted in the direction of Parma, hoping, perhaps, to draw the Tuscans out of the hills and onto more level ground. If this was his intention, he was unsuccessful; he turned suddenly, marching directly on Canossa. Matilda's intelligence kept her well informed of the emperor's movements, and as the German column advanced on the castle through a dense fog, the garrisons of both Bianello and Canossa sallied out and fell upon the enemy from two sides. The surprise was complete; the imperial standard was captured, and Henry was forced to beat a hasty retreat, pursued as far as the Po by the victorious Tuscans. There is no indication of the size of the forces involved in this action, but it does credit to the generalship of Matilda, who is said to have been educated in the military arts by her father. She knew strategy and tactics and could ride and wield a battle-axe with manly skill.

By the end of the eleventh century, warfare of a feudal nature was rapidly disappearing in northern Italy. In the more remote and backward areas of the Alps and the Apennines, feudal wars continued much as before, but these were archaic in comparison with developments in the Lombard plain. Here the feudal magnates fought, to be sure, but in a losing struggle against the thriving and increasingly powerful cities. As it turned out, once the rural nobles were subjected to the authority of the towns, their military capabilities were utilized to further civic ambitions. Unfortunately, urban energies were largely frittered away in bitter intercity rivalries that often degenerated into open hostilities. Had local interest not interfered, the Italians of the Po Valley might well have put together a powerful state during the Middle Ages. The broad Lombard plain was ideally suited for cavalry operations, and under ordinary circumstances, cavalry enjoyed a considerable advantage over infantry when fighting on level ground. The nobles, trained to mounted combat, were essential components of the armies of the communes during the eleventh and twelfth centuries. Only the nobles and the wealthier urban classes could afford the expense of horse and armor, and only they could afford to put in the time necessary to master the technique of fighting on horseback. The mass levy of citizens was thus dependent on the nobles for security in the field.

The strengths and weaknesses of the communal military system are well illustrated by the campaign of 1160 and the resulting battle of Carcano. The Milanese, with the full levy of four of the six *portae*, or quarters, of the city (presumably two-thirds of the city's military force), had laid siege to the Comasque castle of Carcano, in the Brianza Valley north of Monza. The Milanese were also supported by contingents from Brescia which included some mounted troops. Emperor Frederick I, who was then in Italy, marched at once to relieve his ally's stronghold. In addition to a considerable number of German heavy horse, the imperial army included units from Como, Novara, Vercelli, and Pavia, the levies of the marquisate of Montferrat, and of the nobles of the Milanese *contado* who were still fighting to preserve their independence against the commune. Frederick was successful in getting his army across his enemy's supply line. His success gave the Milanese the unpleasant choice of surrendering or of fighting their way out. The latter course was chosen.

The order of battle cannot be completely reconstructed, but apparently the German knights were opposed to the infantry of Milan, while the emperor's Italian allies faced the Milanese and Brescian horsemen. The charge of the imperial horse broke the infantry of Milan; the *carroccio* was reached, and the great standard of the city was captured. On the other wing, however, the knights of Brescia and Milan crushed the contingents of Como and Vercelli and nearly destroyed that of Novara. Then, instead of engaging in a reckless pursuit, as was frequently done in medieval battles, the victorious knights turned to aid the hard-pressed infantry opposed to the Germans. The onset of the Milanese and Brescians compelled the now outnumbered forces of the emperor to withdraw. Frederick took refuge in the castle of Baradello, but he had to abandon his prisoners and a considerable amount of booty. On the next day the victors met and defeated a column of troops from Lodi and Cremona who were marching to join the imperial army. Success on the battlefield was largely negated, however, when the garrison of Carcano made a sortie in force and destroyed all the Milanese siege engines. This setback forced the raising of the siege and the return of the army to Milan.

Although the Carcano campaign is not as well known or as well documented as that of Legnano sixteen years later, it has several points of interest that merit attention because they foreshadow Legnano, which is analyzed in a later chapter. In 1160 the Italian infantry had not yet acquired the experience and confidence which enabled it to play so decisive a role in 1176. Yet it is noteworthy that despite the loss of the *carroccio,* its resistance continued long enough for the cavalry to win the fight on its part of the field and then intervene successfully against the German knights, as it was to do again at Legnano. At Carcano the decisive arm was still the heavy mailed cavalry. Even though the division was composite—made up of troopers from Milan and Brescia—its commanders seem to have had their men well under control. Not always, even in more modern and better disciplined armies, have cavalrymen been able to restrain the impulse to pursue a beaten enemy for many miles. That they were able to resist the impulse at Carcano and to go immediately to the aid of the infantry reflects credit on the troops and their commanders.

The most characteristic element of warfare in twelfth-century Lombardy was the siege of castles and walled towns. Owing to the large number of cities with the resources to pursue an independent course, their close proximity to one another, and the intense rivalries between cities, interurban wars were almost continuous. One such persistent feud involved Milan and Como, which controlled the trade routes north from Milan over the Alps. In 1118 a Milanese force, complete with *carroccio,* launched an attack on Como, but found its way barred by apparently the full Comasque levy at Baradello, some two miles south of the city. Action was joined, but no decision had been reached when darkness brought a halt to hostilities.

During the night the Milanese marched around the flank of the Comasque army and assaulted the city, now denuded of defenders. Entry was gained, but the troops dispersed in search of plunder. In the morning Comasque lookouts on nearby hills spotted smoke from fires set in the city. Forming up in haste, they marched home, fell upon the unsuspecting Milanese, and inflicted a total defeat upon the traditional enemy. With varying details, accounts of such engagements could be repeated almost indefinitely.

Added to the inflammable intercity rivalries were the attempts of successive Holy Roman emperors to revive imperial authority in the Po Valley—attempts in which the imperial cause was supported by some cities and opposed by others. These led to the heavy fortification of all important cities and of many smaller towns and to the development of siegecraft well in advance of that north of the Alps. An example—one of literally scores that might be cited—is the siege of Crema by Emperor Frederick I in 1159–1160. Frederick's ultimate objective in Lombardy was the subjection of Milan, but in spite of reinforcements from Germany, he was still in insufficient strength to launch a direct attack on the city. Instead, he was persuaded by the Cremonese to lay siege to Crema, one of Milan's staunchest allies.

Crema was a small town, and although it was fortified by a wall and a deep, wide ditch and possessed a citadel of considerable strength, the emperor apparently thought that he could speedily reduce it. On the contrary, the siege which opened in July lasted for nearly seven months. The townsmen who manned the walls were reinforced by auxiliaries from Milan and Brescia, food supplies were ample, and the garrison offered a stubborn resistance. Both sides were guilty of atrocities, common occurrences at this time. Engineers of the imperial army constructed a large movable tower of several stories which was to be rolled up to the walls. When it was close enough, a bridge was to be lowered, and troops stationed within the tower would rush across and sieze possession of a section of the wall. Reinforcements could then be brought up in safety. Such towers had been used with success, notably by the Crusaders at Jerusalem in 1099. They were, of course, constructed of wood, and vulnerable to fire as well as to stones cast by enemy artillery stationed on the walls. In order to get his tower up to the walls of Crema, Frederick had hostages from Milan and Crema fastened to the front of it in the expectation that the defenders would hold their fire. But the garrison shot anyway, and although some of the unfortunate hostages were slain, the accurate fire of the engines on the city wall so damaged the tower that it had to be hauled back out of range.

After more than six months of applying constant pressure, the besiegers were finally successful in getting towers close enough to the wall to lower the bridges. Covered by archers stationed in the upper levels, picked troops rushed across to the city wall. Although numerous casualties were inflicted on the defenders, attack after attack was beaten off. At the end of the day's fighting, however, losses were found to be so great that the outer circuit of the walls was abandoned, and the remaining defenders retired into the citadel. Counsels concluded that successful resistance was now out of the question, and negotiations were opened for the surrender of the city. By twelfth-century standards the terms offered were quite lenient. The inhabitants of Crema were permitted to depart with whatever possessions they could carry; the Brescian and Milanese auxiliaries escaped only with their lives. The town was then burned, and its territory was granted to Cremona.

The reduction of Crema occupied more than the normal campaigning season. The duration of the siege had long since exhausted the obligatory service of the German feudatories, most of whom returned home, and the remaining German troops were too few for serious operations against Milan. The emperor withdrew to Pavia to await reinforcements.

The meager accomplishments of the campaign emphasize the major military problem of the emperors who attempted to extend their authority south of the Alps. Imperial power in Lombardy rested on an insecure foundation at best, and military success depended more, perhaps, on the efforts of Italian partisans than on armies marched across the Brenner. Cities such as Pavia served as bases for operations; their territories provided essential supplies and provisions; their troops regularly augmented the German contingents and often continued to serve after the imperial troops had departed. Should the Lombard cities, or even a considerable fraction of them, ever unite against the emperor, it is obvious—with the hindsight of eight centuries—that he would have a difficult time in reducing any one of them. With no fortified base, with no sure source of supply, and with no local allies, a purely German army would be unable to make much head against the opposition of city after city. The current state of the military art gave the defenders a tremendous advantage over the besiegers, and famine was the only sure way to reduce a resolutely defended town. Although emperors never failed to find Italian allies, more than a score of cities signed as anti-imperialists at the pacification of Venice in

1177, and an imperial army could never be held together long enough to make even a dent in the anti-imperialist front. In addition to the limitations on military service, the Germans also had to contend with an unfamiliar climate and the inevitable outbreak of disease due to a lack of even rudimentary sanitation in the camps. Usually, if a city could hold out for six months—Crema was an exception in this respect—the defenders could reasonably hope that the enemy would be compelled to raise the siege as a result of the operation of purely natural causes. The formation of the Lombard League in 1167 marked the beginning of the end for imperial pretensions in Italy; Legnano simply marked the point of no return.

The military history of northern Italy from the late eighth century to the end of the twelfth shows the failure of military feudalism to take root, in spite of seemingly favorable conditions. Lombard military institutions were not incompatible with those of the Franks, and Carolingian capitularies made little distinction between Franks and Lombards. Frankish margraves and counts seemed to succeed Lombard dukes and *gastaldii* with no serious effect on military organization and efficiency. Armies commanded by Franks but made up primarily of Lombards won notable victories as far afield as the plains of the Danube. Even after the collapse of the Carolingian administration in the ninth century, the ephemeral kings of Italy relied largely on feudal levies in their wars against Moslems, Hungarians, and the numerous contenders for the crown. Although immunities were granted to the magnates on a vast scale, they differed little in magnitude from those granted by or extorted from the later Carolingians and early Capetians in Frankish Gaul. The magnates themselves, especially those in the frontier marquisates such as Friuli, Ivrea, and Tuscany, seemed as well established as their contemporaries in Poitou, Bavaria, or Flanders at the end of the tenth century. A hundred years later military feudalism was virtually obsolete, except in the more remote and inaccessible parts of the Marches, Tuscany, and the Alpine foothills. Elsewhere the feudal tenants were fighting a rear-guard action against the rising power of the towns, and before the twelfth century had run its course the nobles of the *contado* had become subject to the communal authorities.

The result was a profound modification in military organization and methods in most of the Lombard plain and in Tuscany. The campaigns of Henry IV against his rebellious vassals in Italy had been typically feudal campaigns, but within a century Frederick I saw all his hopes of an imperial revival shattered on the field of Legnano. In the interim, towns had come under the control of their leading citizens, the urban nobles and the wealthier mercantile families. The subjection of the feudal nobles of the *contado* to the commune enabled the cities to build military organizations of considerable efficiency for their day. Hardened in the almost continuous interurban wars, the combination of horse and foot developed by the Lombard towns was more than a match for anything that could be brought across the Alps to fight against it. Unfortunately, the Lombard League did not lead to a northern Italian confederation, and though it was able to prevent outside domination, the great energies of the cities were expended in countless internecine wars which so weakened the communes that they fell an easy prey to tyrants in the fourteenth century and became helpless pawns on the European chessboard in the sixteenth.

8

Military Feudalism
in Germany

Any attempt to discuss the impact of feudalism on the military institutions of Germany is likely to become an exercise in futility. The reason is that Germany, in what Ganshof describes as the "classic" age of feudal institutions, was only superficially feudalized.[1] In Lotharingia (Lorraine), in Franconia, in Burgundy, and to a lesser extent in Bavaria—all of which had come within the orbit of the Carolingian empire—feudal practices had taken root and distinctly influenced military developments. The Rhineland, the very heart of the old Frankish state, was, as might be expected, the most thoroughly feudalized. Here the lord-vassal relationship was most explicitly defined, and here the traditional appurtenances of feudalism— knight service and the castle—were most completely developed. Elsewhere, and particularly in the north and east, the picture becomes more confused. As late as Bouvines (1214), a large proportion of the Saxon contingent was still fighting on foot.

[1] F. L. Ganshof, *Feudalism*, trans. Philip Grierson (2d Eng. ed,; New York, 1961), pp. 65–68.

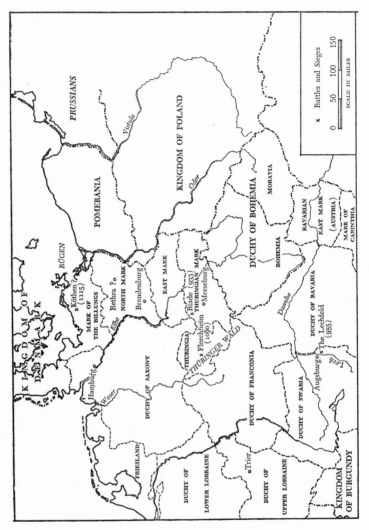

Map 6. Germany ca. 1050

The end of the Carolingian dynasty in Germany (911) brought less of the confusion that prevailed in Italy and Gaul under similar circumstances. The establishment of the strong Saxon dynasty in 919 and its revival of an effective royal administrative apparatus were factors which tended to slow the spread of feudal institutions. But there were other elements which must also be considered in showing why Germany, until the middle of the twelfth century, cannot be called a feudal state. The existence of numerous and extensive allodial estates, as in southern France and in Spain, helps explain why German society was less feudalized than that of neighboring Capetian France. The feudal relationship applied only to certain estates and to particular individuals, so that even among the noble class there were many legal bonds that were outside the feudal framework. More important was the effective survival, long after its abandonment in much of western Europe, of the obligation of all free men to perform military service. The distinction between those who fought and those who tilled the soil was slow in developing, and as late as the thirteenth century free peasants were still to be found in German armies.

The existence of an open frontier to the east was a factor in the preservation of a free peasantry with military obligations. Early in the tenth century, Henry the Fowler (919–936), the first of the Saxon kings, established fortified posts (*Burgen*) along the Saxon and Thuringian frontiers. The defense of these posts was provided by groups of nine men, one of whom stayed permanently within the walls, at this stage doubtless of wood. The other eight tilled fields located in the vicinity of the fort and reported for duty only when attack threatened. Thus the "defenders of the Saxon border were themselves genuine peasants, cultivating the soil with their own hands—*agrarii milites*." [2] The easternmost, and hence most exposed, of these frontier posts was Merseburg; to encourage settlement, Henry gave every able-bodied thief who was apprehended the choice of hanging or going to live at Merseburg. Considerable turbulence probably characterized frontier life, but Merseburg soon became a bulwark on the eastern borderlands.

In Saxony itself, for centuries the army consisted of the levy of all free men, the old Germanic *Heerban*. The only differentiation was between noble and nonnoble free men. All alike fought on foot, and there was nothing comparable to the *ordo militaris* (the knightly order) of more feudalized lands. In spite of the attempts of Henry the Fowler to persuade the Saxon and Thuringian nobles to fight on horseback, Saxon infantry appeared in most of the important operations of the eleventh century. Elsewhere in the kingdom, feudalism of a sort had begun to affect military organization. Yet it is noteworthy that with few exceptions the grants of benefices in return for military service that survive from the eleventh century were made in the old Frankish lands, such as Lotharingia, Franconia, and Burgundy; not until the twelfth century was a German vassal customarily rewarded with a fief. Even in those lands where feudal practices were more common there were variations from the usual pattern. In 1076 the count of Hainaut, as a vassal of the bishop of Liége, was obligated to answer the summons to military duty with all his forces, horse and foot.

[2] Marc Bloch, *Feudal Society*, trans. L. A. Manyon (Chicago, 1961), p. 180.

Another factor which differentiated Germany from other feudal lands was the extraordinary role played by the church and churchmen in military affairs. Of course the fighting bishop or abbot was by no means uncommon in feudal Europe; Bishop Odo of Bayeux galloping about the field at Hastings armed with a club—since churchmen were forbidden to shed blood—is a familiar figure. Most church lands, except those held in free alms, were held on military tenure; the Norman kings of England drew perhaps as much as 15 per cent of their knight service from ecclesiastical tenants. But on the basis of admittedly scanty evidence, it seems that the German kings relied principally on the contingents of the German hierarchy in forming their armies. The reasons are fairly clear. Given the weakness of the central administrative system and the unreliability of the great crown vassals, particularly the dukes, the kings looked increasingly to the church for support during the tenth and eleventh centuries. Churchmen, the only literate class, staffed the rudimentary civil service; faithful performance of duty was usually rewarded with ecclesiastical preferment. Thus the German hierarchy was composed of men who owed place and privilege to the king and who were more likely to be loyal than the lay nobles who sought only their own advantage. As late as the reign of Frederick I (1152–1190), it was said, doubtless with exaggeration, that not a single German bishop could be cited for his spiritual qualities and that hardly a single one was not a politician or a soldier, or both. These trusted servants were granted the authority of counts even in districts beyond their own diocesan boundaries in an effort to curb the power of the great magnates.

An example from the reign of Henry II (1002–1024)

will serve to illustrate the use made of the church by the German kings. Henry's brother-in-law, Adalberon, was perhaps typical of the nobility of the day—headstrong, quarrelsome, and predatory. He ravaged the archdiocese of Trier without mercy, reducing the countryside to a wilderness and compelling the archbishop to seek refuge in Coblenz. To curb the activities of Adalberon, King Henry selected a tough-minded young Franconian baron, Poppo of Bamberg. He was rushed through the grades of the clergy, soon emerging as archbishop of Trier. The new archbishop distributed sixty prebends of his see as benefices to sixty knights; leading his own troops, Poppo soon captured Adalberon's castles.

Just as the German kings relied on ecclesiastical support to maintain some semblance of internal order, so they depended on the contingents of the church to supply the armies which fought in Italy, on the eastern frontiers, and against rebellious subjects. One warrior priest was Udalrich, bishop of Augsburg from 924 to 973. He strengthened the walls of his episcopal city to withstand Magyar assaults. His military units and those of the bishop of Chur supported Otto I (936–973) against his rebellious son Liudolf in 954. A year later he took a prominent part in the defense of Augsburg against the Hungarians and in the ensuing engagement at the Lechfeld. The often cited Italian expedition of Otto II (973–983) in 980–981 found twenty-nine ecclesiastical tenants supplying more than twice as many troops as the twenty-one lay magnates who accompanied the column. Emperor Henry III (1039–1056) was joined by three archbishops, ten bishops, two abbots, and their troops on his Italian expedition of 1046. The Italian campaigns of Frederick I were fought largely by armies composed of church contingents and commanded by churchmen such as Archbishop Christian of Mainz. Thus the military burdens on the church were heavy, owing largely to royal suspicions about the loyalty of the lay nobles. Bishoprics and royal monasteries from the Alps to the North Sea and from the Meuse to the Elbe provided the largest and most reliable part of the royal army.

The contributions of the church militant were not the only sources of military manpower. The king still had the right, in theory at least, to summon all his subjects to military service (*clamor patriae*, "the call to the country"). In the ninth and tenth centuries the general levy of each great duchy marched under the command of its duke, but it seems that the *Heerban* was summoned for the last time in 910, with results that are discussed later. By the eleventh century the general summons was in use only in the eastern frontier districts, where Slavic raids were frequent. In those areas where feudal institutions had become established, the dukes and counts of the whole kingdom were obliged to appear at the muster with their retainers, and with notable exceptions in times of rebellion, the obligation was generally met. This made possible the great Italian expeditions. It was the breakdown of this system—the refusal of some of the great magnates to accompany Frederick I to Italy—that led directly to the defeat at Legnano in 1176 and the end of Barbarossa's dream of empire. As Bloch succinctly put it:

It is not really surprising that this government which had no taxation other than the few financial "services" of the churches, no salaried officials, no permanent army—this nomadic government which possessed no convenient means of communication and which men felt to be physically and morally remote from them, should not always succeed in ensuring the obedience of its subjects. No reign in fact was free from rebellions.[3]

Apart from the bishops and the abbots of royal foundations, there were relatively few real military vassals—nobles who held lands in return for military service—and most of these were to be found in lands subject to French influence. There was, however, another source of military manpower in Germany which had no counterpart anywhere else in feudal Europe. There evolved a class of unfree administrators and warriors known as *ministeriales*. This new class of officials appeared first in the reign of Henry the Fowler, but they did not begin to assume significance until the time of Conrad II (1024–1039). Their use offered obvious advantages, not only to the king, but to the magnates, both lay and ecclesiastical. The *ministeriales* originated in a favored class of serfs who were not bound to the soil, except in theory. At first they were probably armed domestics, but they were gradually installed in minor administrative and military offices that were supported from manorial revenues.

Both lay and ecclesiastical magnates preferred to raise troops in this way instead of alienating their lands as fiefs held on military tenure. This approach to raising military quotas was especially favored by churchmen. In France and in Norman England, bishops, abbots, and an occasional abbess provided their knight service by granting fiefs to knights, but the German ecclesiastics were reluctant to do this. Once a knight was established on the land, it had to become hereditary in his family, and the lord could evict him only by force, even though he had not

[3] Bloch, *Feudal Society*, p. 427.

performed his military service. An unfree soldier could have no claim whatever against his lord, and what had been granted for his support could easily be withdrawn. Moreover, since a serf-knight (other unfree soldiers served as infantry) owed his relatively privileged condition to his lord, he was more apt to serve faithfully and he was less likely to connive against his patron than a member of the knightly order. These considerations appealed to lay nobles as well as to kings and bishops, and *ministeriales* became a permanent and important component in all German armies, especially after the normal feudal service began to decline in effectiveness.

The *ministerialis*, while remaining a serf in law, came to enjoy the rights and privileges of the petty noble—to the intense disgust of the latter—and eventually he was absorbed into the petty nobility, either through distinguished military service or by assuming *Ritter* status. By the twelfth century the *ministeriales* began to imitate the nobles and to build castles on lands they had usurped. One important *ministerialis*, Werner of Bolland, is said, probably with exaggeration, to have owned seventeen castles and claimed the homage of 1,100 knights. At any rate, by the beginning of the century, the formation of the class was complete. The ecclesiastical contingents that marched in royal and imperial armies were largely composed of *ministeriales*.

In most of feudal Europe castle-guard was regarded as a knightly obligation in addition to field service. In Germany, until the mid-twelfth century, the obligations were sharply differentiated. Castles began to appear in Germany perhaps toward the end of the tenth century, but extensive castle-building seems to date primarily from the

eleventh century, when numerous motte-and-bailey structures were erected in the Rhineland, where French influence was always strong. Fortifications, as in France and
Norman England, were typically of earth and timber, but
by the end of the century, Henry IV (1056–1106) was
building stone castles in Saxony and Thuringia. The archi-
tect, or planner, of these castles was an ecclesiastic, Bishop
Benno II of Osnabrück, the earliest known military engineer of medieval Germany. The defense of these castles
was entrusted to garrisons composed of *ministeriales* from
Bavaria and Swabia, who were thoroughly detested by the
Saxons because of their arrogant and turbulent conduct.
Castle-guard, apparently, was not a knightly obligation in
Germany as it was elsewhere. Not only royal castles, but
those of lay and ecclesiastical magnates, were held by
ministeriales.

Other sources of military manpower are referred to
occasionally in contemporary accounts. Townsmen, especially in the Rhineland and on the eastern frontier, are
most frequently mentioned. By the early eleventh century wooden palisades were giving way to more permanent
fortifications of stone in such places as Magdeburg, Pader-
born, Worms, and Verden. The burghers of the Rhineland
towns, favored by imperial charters, were loyal supporters
of the central authority against both church and nobles.
In 1080, for example, their contingents were prominent in
the armies with which Henry IV defeated the forces of
the counterking, Rudolf of Swabia. But although they frequently participated in the civil disorders that were common in Germany and often had to stand siege behind their
walls, there is no evidence that the burghers took part in
military expeditions beyond the borders of the country.

By the middle of the twelfth century reference is made to a class of sergeants (*servientes*). Modern authorities generally assume that these were mounted soldiers, more lightly armed than the knights, although in France, England, and Syria some of the sergeants were certainly infantry. It is not possible to determine whether the *serviens* was a type of *ministerialis* or, if he was not, on what basis he was obliged to render military service. He may even have been a mercenary, but references to mercenaries are ambiguous. Perhaps the four thousand knights promised by Henry III to the Milanese popular leader Lanzone in the 1040's were mercenaries, but it is equally likely that they were *ministeriales*. The scarcity of references to mercenaries in German annals is probably due to the availability of unfree troops who could be posted at any time to any place.

It is virtually impossible to get any idea of how the various contingents were organized or how they were brigaded for the march or on the battlefield. For very few engagements can one reconstruct the order of battle with any confidence. The campaigns fought by German armies during the feudal period fall into three main groups: campaigns waged against foreign invaders; campaigns against the Slavic peoples on the eastern frontier; and the great expeditions into Italy which bulk large in medieval historiography but which were politically and militarily futile. The wars against outside aggressors virtually ended with Otto the Great's smashing defeat of the Magyars at the Lechfeld in 955. The border wars east of the Elbe, which continued well beyond the period covered in this survey, were of considerable importance in the long contest between Slavs and Germans and in the general history of border warfare between peoples of different cultural levels. In ferocity, these wars are similar to those waged along the advancing frontier in North America from the seventeenth to the early nineteenth century. The Italian expeditions received the most publicity, but although they too continued into the post feudal period, imperial ambitions were shattered at Legnano in 1176, one of the truly decisive engagements of the Middle Ages. In addition, chronic civil wars marked every reign. These were more similar to the so-called feudal wars that occurred elsewhere in Europe than to the campaigns in Italy and along the eastern borders.

The last really important invasion of Europe prior to the appearance of the Mongols in the thirteenth century was that of the Magyars. Although they first came to the attention of western writers as early as 862, they did not permanently establish themselves in the valleys of the Danube and Theiss until the closing years of the century. The Hungarians (Magyars) were a nation of horse archers, typical Asian nomads. Their greatest asset was their mobility, especially in comparison with the Frankish levies of slow-moving infantry and feudal horse. In hand-to-hand combat, which they engaged in reluctantly, they were no match for the taller, more strongly built Germans. They did not generally attack fortified places.

After they had settled on the borders of the East Frankish state, they subjected western Europe for the next half-century to a series of devastating raids that carried westward beyond the Rhine and southward beyond the Alps. The unfortunate campaign of King Berenger I of Italy has already been discussed. The German experience was little happier. The general levy of the East Franks was called into the field only once during the reign of the last Carolingian, Ludwig the Child (899–911). On this occasion (910), the Germans, marching in three separated columns, were unable to effect a junction, and three different actions were fought several miles apart. The main body, under the nominal command of the young King Ludwig, encamped the night before the battle near Augsburg, on the river Lech. The Magyars launched a predawn attack which apparently surprised the Germans. There followed a fight in which the usual Hungarian strategems were employed. After a show of resistance to the German counterattack, the Magyars began a retreat which was successful in drawing the enemy into an ambush. The king's army was struck on the flanks and from the rear by troops charging from ambush, as the retreating units simultaneously wheeled about and poured volleys of arrows into the disordered German front. The victory was complete, and for the next decade Germany, wracked by civil war, lay open to Hungarian marauders.

The fortress-building policy of Henry the Fowler helped render the eastern frontier more secure, but vast Magyar raids in 924, 926, and 954 penetrated into France, Burgundy, and Lombardy. Henry also attempted to persuade the Saxons and Thuringians to learn to fight on horseback. His efforts were not completely successful, but when the Magyars, in 933, after a nine years' truce resumed their attacks on Germany, they found the border studded with new fortified posts, and the newly mounted local levies were able to catch up with and destroy the marauding bands.

To guard against the principal enemy column, King Henry kept his main army behind the frontier, and to aid

the Saxons and Thuringians, he called up mounted contingents from the neighboring duchies of Franconia and
Bavaria. With these troops the king treated the Hungarians to a dose of their own medicine. The bulk of his cavalry was concealed in ambush; only the levy of Thuringia
with a few knights could be seen by the advancing Hungarians, who were thus induced to attack. The Bavarian
and Franconian horse charged suddenly from ambush and
took the enemy completely by surprise. Without waiting
for the Germans to come to close quarters, the Magyars
broke and fled. While a few were cut down in the pursuit
and many more were drowned in the Unstrut which lay
across their line of retreat, most of the invaders got off
safely. This engagement was fought at Riade and is generally called the battle of Merseburg, although the actual
fighting took place nearer to Erfurt than to any other
town.

The decisive defeat of the Hungarians, however, had to
wait another twenty-two years. The victory of Otto I at
the Lechfeld (10 August 955) is important not only because it removed the Hungarian threat, but also because
the unusual amount of recorded detail provides a better
insight into the strategy and tactics employed by feudal
generals than is ordinarily obtainable. In 955 the Magyars,
in contrast to their usual practice, laid siege to the episcopal city of Augsburg, whose defenses were in the hands of
the venerable but competent Bishop Udalrich. To understand fully the ensuing operations, it is necessary to know
something about the terrain in the vicinity of Augsburg.
The medieval city was located in the angle formed by the
junction of the river Wertach with the river Lech, just
north of the walls, and it seems that south of the town the

west bank of the Lech was higher than the east. Although opinion is not unanimous, most modern authorities assert that the Magyars had encamped south of Augsburg, between the Wertach and the Lech.

They had timed the invasion shrewdly, for King Otto had just subdued a major rebellion, and there was still unrest in Lotharingia, the center of the revolt. Moreover, the Slavs on the lower Elbe were restless; therefore Saxon participation in any military operations would be limited. King Otto, although he could count on only a fraction of the military strength of the kingdom, immediately called out all available forces. The result must have been disappointing; for the relief of Augsburg the king is said to have mustered about 8000 men, all mounted—a not impossible number at that time and place. There were no contingents from Lotharingia, and only a comparative handful from Saxony, Thuringia, and Franconia. The majority of the troopers came from Bavaria and Swabia; there were in addition the king's personal following and a modest force of Czechs under the command of Boleslav of Bohemia. The army was brigaded in eight divisions (called *legiones* in the anachronistic style of the chronicler): three Bavarian, two Swabian, one Franconian, commanded by Duke Conrad, and one Bohemian under Prince Boleslav; the eighth division, made up of the personal following of the king and such Saxons and Thuringians as had managed to reach the muster, was somewhat larger than the others and was commanded by Otto in person. Each division had a strength of about 1000 men. Without waiting for further reinforcements, Otto marched to raise the siege of Augsburg.

What considerations led to the king's decision regarding

the approach march? He may have recalled or have been reminded that his father's victory at Riade in 933 was incomplete because the Magyars had an open line of retreat once they had crossed the Unstrut and because the bigger Germans in their heavier armor and on their slower horses had not been able to catch up with the more mobile Hungarians. At any rate, he acted as though these considerations had influenced his movements. Instead of marching directly on Augsburg from the north or northwest, he apparently marched across to the north of the city and came down on the east side of the Lech, squarely astride the Magyars' line of retreat to their homeland. Although the terrain east of the Lech is generally suitable for the harassing tactics employed by the light cavalry masses of the Magyars, Otto was able to move through some broken ground, to encamp some distance behind the river, and to deploy without molestation.

When the Hungarians learned of the approach of the relieving army, they lifted the siege of Augsburg, deposited their excess gear in camp, and crossed the Lech to meet the enemy. The battle on the Lech is one of the few early medieval engagements in which the order of battle can be determined with reasonable accuracy. The king deployed his army in a single line. On the German left were the two Swabian divisions; next, Otto's own command (his retinue, plus the Saxons and Thuringians); then the three Bavarian divisions. The Franconians under Duke Conrad held the extreme right. The Bohemians, because either their trustworthiness or their military competence was doubtful, were posted to guard the baggage and the camp. The deployment seems to have been hardly completed when the Magyars, who had crossed the Lech much sooner than expected, were seen advancing to the attack all along the German front. There was apparently no order, just a formless, ever shifting mass of men and horses. The hundred thousand Magyar horsemen of the chroniclers can have no basis in fact, but the knights in the German line can be excused for thinking there were so many.

This was only a holding attack, for part of the Hungarian army, out of sight of the German line, had slipped around a flank—which one is not known—and pounced upon the Bohemians guarding the camp and baggage. The latter, after only a brief resistance, broke and fled. The victorious Magyars then charged in on the rear of the two Swabian divisions already engaged in front. This unexpected attack threw the left wing into disorder, and it began to recoil to the right on King Otto's center division. The flexibility of the German formation was amply demonstrated, for although there was no tactical reserve, the king was able to disengage the division on the extreme right and move it across behind the line to aid the distressed Swabians. Conrad, the commander of the Franconian division, had been involved in the recent rebellion and had a reputation to redeem. He brought the Franconians in with a rush that completely overwhelmed the Magyars, who then attempted to rejoin their main body.

The king meanwhile had been watching the action on his left. With his own division and those of the Bavarians he held off the rest of the Hungarians, while Conrad disposed of the enemy diversion and restored some order in the left of the line. Then Otto ordered a general advance all along the front. The Hungarians, already shaken by the failure of the outflanking maneuver, had little inclination to stand and fight. As is noted above, the smaller, less well-armed Magyars were no match for the Germans, man to man. After firing a few ineffectual volleys of arrows, the Hungarians turned and made for their camp. The Germans followed hard on the heels of the enemy, slaying many. Others were drowned in the Lech as they tried to urge their tired horses up the steep and slippery west bank. The Magyar camp was taken and plundered the same day, and remnants of the invading host were relentlessly pursued for the two days following the battle. With Otto's army barring the direct line of retreat, the Hungarians had to make a great sweep south and east in order to get home, and small bands were intercepted and destroyed by the Bavarian peasants as they attempted to make their escape.

Casualty figures were not accurately kept in the tenth century, so it is not known how severe the German losses were. It may be guessed that the Swabians suffered heavily during the opening phase of the conflict. Duke Conrad was slain by a chance shot, but he had certainly redeemed his good name; his prompt intervention, which involved what, for those days, was a complicated maneuver, probably was the decisive factor in the battle. The conduct of the campaign on both the strategic and tactical levels marks King Otto as probably the best general of his day. And the conclusion must be that heavy horse, when properly handled, was superior to any other force available to western European commanders in the tenth century.

For nearly six centuries, German kings pursued imperial ambitions which resulted in a large number of military expeditions into Italy. Their impact on the development of Italian military institutions and practices has already been discussed; the effects on Germany were equally significant. The dissipation of royal resources in the vain pursuit of

imperial grandeur fostered the independence of the territorial nobility; the manpower losses through battle and
disease weakened the material ability of the kings to control the great feudatories; and the long, bitter struggle
with the church deprived the king of the support of the
powerful German hierarchy.

It is impossible, of course, to estimate with reasonable
accuracy the composition of the armies which the various
kings led across the Alps. Allegations that, in 1111, Henry
II had 30,000 men or that in 1158, Frederick I commanded 15,000 horse and 100,000 foot may be dismissed
as fabrications. There is, however, one bit of evidence, dating from the late tenth century, which makes some informed guesses possible. In 980, Otto II conducted an
army across the Alps to campaign against the Moslems of
southern Italy. In the autumn of the following year he sent
back to Germany for reinforcements, since he had also
become involved in hostilities with the Byzantines. Chance
has preserved what is almost certainly the list of heavy
cavalry contingents that were mustered in response to the
imperial summons. Classified according to place of origin,
these troops came from three areas: Franconia, Lotharingia, and Bavaria-Swabia. The Franconian units were provided by ten ecclesiastical and fourteen lay tenants; the
Lotharingians were supplied by six nobles and seven prelates; and the Bavarian-Swabian contingents came entirely
from ecclesiastical sources. All told, four archbishops, fifteen bishops, and ten abbots furnished 1,482 troops to the
expedition, while two dukes, six counts, two margraves,
and twelve lesser nobles provided either 638 or 648, for a
total of either 2,080 or 2,090 men.

It will be noted that even at this early date the ecclesiastical contribution was more than double that of the lay magnates. It should also be noted that no infantry are mentioned, and—what is more important—no troops were provided by the tenants in Saxony, Thuringia, Frisia, and the border margraviates. The most probable explanation is that the contingents from these lands had marched with the emperor in the previous year. It must not be supposed that the nearly 2,000 heavy cavalry represented the full levy of the lands involved. The figure does, however, give a clue to the size of German mounted potential. Lot estimates that the total mounted service due the king in the mid-twelfth century was approximately 6000 knights, and states that it would be impossible to support more than half that number on an Italian campaign.[4]

Most of the campaigns conducted by German kings in Italy during the eleventh and early twelfth centuries were concentrated in the vicinity of Rome and in Tuscany. The fact that the levies of the Tuscan marquisate were able to fight Henry IV to a standstill is another indication of the modest forces brought south by German commanders. With the accession of Frederick I to the throne of Germany and the Holy Roman Empire in 1152, and the determination of that monarch to impose imperial authority on the Lombard towns, the character of warfare changed. The lengthy and often futile sieges in which Frederick engaged have been noted in a previous chapter; the fate of imperial ambitions was not, however, decided in the siege

[4] Ferdinand Lot, *L'Art Militaire et les Armées au Moyen Age en Europe et dans le Proche Orient* (2 vols; Paris, 1946), II, 159–167. Lot is perhaps low in his estimates, for it seems unlikely that knight service due in twelfth-century Germany would scarcely exceed that of eleventh-century England.

lines but on the field of Legnano, which revealed both the strength of the league of Lombard cities and the weakness of the German military structure.

After an absence of several years, Frederick invaded Italy in the autumn of 1174, crossing the Mont Cenis Pass, since the other, more direct routes were held by cities of the Lombard League. After preliminary operations the emperor settled down to an unsuccessful siege of Alessandria that was not abandoned until April of the following year. Frederick then retired to Pavia, where he spent the balance of 1175 and the early part of 1176 raiding the lands of members of the League. To the south, his viceroy, the capable Archbishop Christian of Mainz, captured San Casciano and ravaged the territory of Bologna.

The emperor was also busy attempting to secure large reinforcements from Germany, but the refusal of the most powerful magnate in southern Germany, Henry the Lion, duke of Bavaria, to answer the summons seriously reduced the number of troops that eventually marched in April 1176. Some 500 knights and 1,500 sergeants, or men-at-arms—not a large force even by twelfth-century standards—under the command of Archbishop Philip of Cologne, Conrad, bishop-elect of Worms, and Duke Berthold of Zähringen, arrived at Como about the middle of May after a fatiguing passage of the Alps. Frederick, with an escort of perhaps 500 knights, marched from Pavia, and by a circuitous route, which avoided the neighborhood of Milan, he joined the newly arrived contingents in Como. Apparently he had planned to return to Pavia, where he would be joined by the forces of the imperialist towns and those of the marquis of Montferrat, before undertaking any major operations. Of course it would be necessary to give Milan a wide berth, even though this involved a considerable divergence from the most direct route between Como and Pavia. Although he took the necessary precautions—an advance guard of 300 knights was thrown out ahead of the main body—Frederick made the mistake of cutting in too close to the city, giving the Milanese and their associates in the Lombard League an opportunity to intercept the imperialists. At one point the line of march chosen by the emperor came within twenty miles of Milan; the confederates, operating on what would be called interior lines, made the most of their opportunity.

It is not very difficult to determine the strength of the imperial army. It consisted of the 2000 mounted troops brought over the Alps in April and May, the 500 horse that escorted Frederick from Pavia to Como, and the civic levy of Como, perhaps 500 strong, the only infantry in the column. Probably the infantry were assigned to guard the impedimenta, for there is no mention of them in the ensuing action. It is more difficult to establish the size of the force dispatched by the Lombard League to intercept the imperialists as they marched past Milan to the north and west. The Milanese were not convinced of the approach of German reinforcements until their actual arrival at Como; hence appeals for aid did not go out until mid-May. By the twenty-seventh, the contingents of the nearer League cities, both horse and foot, had concentrated in Milan, and consultations doubtless took place about possible courses of action. It is certain that the forces of the League significantly outnumbered those that Frederick had at his disposal. Milan itself could put 2000 knights into the field. Other mounted troops included 300 from Novara and Vercelli, 200 from Piacenza, and 50 from Lodi. Contingents also came in from Brescia, Verona, and the Veronese mark, but their composition is not specified. It is not unlikely that the League mustered as many as 4000 horse, as opposed to Frederick's 2,500. The Veronese and Brescian infantry were designated to hold Milan, while the Milanese foot soldiers marched out with the mounted troops to intercept the imperial column.

The leaguers seem to have been well served by their intelligence, for on 29 May a force of 700 Lombard knights managed to get across the emperor's line of march and collided with the 300 troopers scouting ahead of his main body, between Busto Arsizio and Borsano. Owing to the wooded character of the terrain, the encounter was a tactical surprise to each party. Although the Germans were outnumbered by more than 2 to 1, they gave ground slowly, giving the main body time to deploy into line of battle, and the Lombards were briskly repulsed when they came up against the main line of resistance. At this juncture, apparently, the Lombard main body began to emerge from the wood and to form up opposite the German line. The Lombard cavalry was organized in four divisions, with all the infantry solidly massed about the *carroccio* of Milan, but the exact order of battle cannot be determined. Despite the fact that the enemy enjoyed great numerical superiority, the action was opened by a charge of the German knights. The impetus of the charge broke up the Lombard cavalry divisions in succession—suggesting that the cavalry had been posted in column of divisions with the infantry in the rear. Many of the defeated knights took flight, some not drawing rein until the walls of Milan were reached. The Milanese cavalry held together, however, and had time to regroup, as the Germans now concentrated their attack on the infantry massed around the *car-roccio*. Slowly the knights began to gain ground against the stubborn Milanese defense, and doubtless they would eventually have gained the day. But the rallied knights of Milan, joined by a body of Brescian horse which had just come on the field, charged into the German flank. The imperial standard went down, the emperor himself was unhorsed and was erroneously reported slain, and German morale collapsed in an instant. It was *sauve-qui-peut* as the imperial army broke up and made for the rear. Many were killed or captured; others were drowned in the river Ticino which lay across the line of retreat to the left rear. The army simply ceased to exist as an organized force, and the survivors, including Frederick himself, made their way singly or in small bands to the shelter of Pavia or Como.

The causes of the disaster can be easily discerned, although its magnitude was the result of the unpredictable panic that seized the German knights. Frederick lacked the strength to force his way past the army of the League. He had no infantry except the levy of Como, and it does not seem to have been committed to action, although it suffered heavily during the flight. Had the emperor enjoyed even numerical equality with the Lombards, he probably could have succeeded, but he could not spare the men to ensure that the Lombard cavalry had no chance to rally. The tenacious resistance of the Lombard infantry which gave the knights another opportunity was the key to the victory. Warfare could no longer be called feudal when armed townsmen could fight heavy cavalry almost to a draw.

The numerous civil wars fought in Germany from the tenth through the twelfth century are only occasionally of military interest, perhaps because so little detail is recorded about them. It might be instructive to know more about the guerrilla campaign waged against Henry IV by Otto of Nordheim in 1070. Otto's operations were centered in the wilderness of the Thüringer Wald and eventually led to more formal civil war. Vast stretches of uncultivated land made irregular operations a practical alternative for the weaker side in any struggle to an extent that was seldom possible in France or England. The military historian would also like to know the details of the winter campaign which culminated in the battle of Florchheim (27 January 1080). Although winter operations were not as rare in the Middle Ages as some writers allege, the action at Florchheim was unusual because of the tactical expedients employed by the contestants, Henry IV and the counterking, Rudolf of Swabia, supported by Saxon rebels. It is not clear whether Otto of Nordheim was cooperating with Rudolf or was operating independently. At any rate, he was in the immediate vicinity.

The encounter took place near the village of Florchheim, between Eisenach and Mülhausen in Thuringia. The armies were separated by a small stream, with the rebels occupying an advantageous position on high ground. All that is known of Henry's army is that it contained Franconians and Bohemians. The king saw that it would be difficult to launch a frontal assault on Rudolf's position, so he decided to try and turn it. He waited to launch his attack until it was dark, which at this season of the year, in this latitude, and with local weather conditions would have been about 4:00 P.M. Henry's attacking column seems to have got across the stream, and the struggle raged fiercely in a heavy snowstorm. One of the king's subordinates, Duke Wratislav of Bohemia, struck down Rudolf's standard bearer, hotly engaged the Saxons, and prompted the counterking to take flight. But on the other side of the stream, it is asserted, Otto of Nordheim surprised and pillaged the royal camp, which had been left poorly guarded, then turned on the Franconians and Bohemians and compelled them to surrender. This turn of events constrained Henry to seek refuge in the Wartburg castle.[5] If this is anything like an accurate description, the action at Florchheim must have been rather wild for a time. This triple battle, if such it was, is unique.

The medieval German *Drang nach Osten* has the fascination that is always attached to frontier warfare. During the tenth century the Germans had pushed across the upper Elbe where the East Mark and Thuringian Mark had been settled. But the lands east of the lower Elbe, heavily forested and often marshy, were still in the hands of pagan Slavic peoples. This area between the Elbe and the Oder was the scene of savage border warfare from the late tenth through the twelfth century. The struggle was not only between the advancing Germans and the Slavs; it involved also the attempts of the church to impose Christianity upon the pagans, which aroused opposition from the Slavs, as well as from the secular magnates, notably the dukes of Saxony, who would lose a considerable amount of tribute if the Slavs were to become Christian and subject to the tithe. The tribute was, in effect, payment for a license to remain heathen. Hence there was bitter con-

---

[5] This is the battle as reconstructed by Lot, who admits that owing to contradictions in the sources, there is much uncertainty about just what happened that snowy evening at Florchheim (*L'Art Militaire,* II, 146–147).

flict, breaking out into actual warfare at times, between the Saxon dukes and the archbishops of Hamburg-Bremen. The Slavs were not united in their opposition to the land-hungry Germans. Some had accepted Christianity, either through genuine conversion or as a matter of self-preservation, but this tended to promote suspicion and hostility among the Slavs themselves. The Germans on one pretext or another pushed eastward beyond the Elbe, establishing strongly fortified posts (*Burgwärde*) at strategic locations, with lesser fortifications in between. The church also joined in the movement, setting up bishoprics at Mecklenburg and Ratzeburg and building monasteries at other places.

It is hardly surprising that the oppressive policies of church and state provoked opposition which at times assumed serious proportions. In 983 and again in 1018 there were massive risings among the trans-Elbian Slavs. On these occasions the eastward march of the Germans was halted and even thrown back, but eventually the more advanced people would resume their inexorable advance. Comparison has been made between the Slavic frontier and the North American Indian frontier in the seventeenth and eighteenth centuries. There was this dissimilarity, however: the German advance against the Slavs was slower because there was less cultural and technological difference between the contestants than there was between the Europeans and the Indians.

The risings of 983 and 1018, which had seriously checked German eastward expansion, were as nothing compared to the Slavic insurrection of 1066. Within a few months most of the *Burgwärde* and the lesser posts were overrun and destroyed. The ecclesiastical establishments were obliterated, the priests were slain, and hundreds of German settlers were carried away into slavery. Even the lands of the archbishopric of Hamburg west of the Elbe were devastated; the castle of Hamburg was captured and its garrison crucified. The surviving Germans fled into the interior. Until the beginning of the twelfth century, the trans-Elbian territory was a Slavic domain where paganism reigned, as the few Christian Slavs returned to the religion of their ancestors.

Although constant raids and counterraids characterized life on the Elbe frontier during the remainder of the eleventh century, it was not until the beginning of the following century that really serious attempts were made to advance German military and ecclesiastical influence beyond the river. The turning point came in 1106, when Lothar of Supplinburg became duke of Saxony after the extinction of the old line of dukes. As a supporter of the church, the new duke was anxious to extend Christianity to the pagan Slavs, and for the first time state and church worked together. But it was a militant Christianity that again began to press eastward. Typical campaigns carried German Christian arms as far east as the Oder in the early twelfth century.

One of the unusual aspects of these operations was that they were always launched during the winter, for this was the only season of the year when the German knights could, with safety, traverse the marshy lands east of the Elbe. In the winter of 1113–1114, for example, in retaliation for a series of devastating raids, an army of 1,600 men, composed of Saxons and Christian Slavs marched northeastward, becoming the first Christian column to cross the river Peene since the time of Otto I. A march of nine days brought the little army to the shores of the Baltic opposite the island of Rügen, the pagan religious center, and the Christians prepared to cross over the ice of the narrow strait that separated the island from the mainland. Only the payment of an enormous tribute saved the shrine from pillage. Two years later, on 9 February 1115, the Slavs were heavily defeated at Köthen by Count Otto of Ballenstadt, and during the winter of 1124–1125, Duke Lothar destroyed the pagan shrine at Rethra. He would also have invaded Rügen had not an inopportune thaw broken up the ice in the strait.

At the end of the first quarter of the twelfth century, the Slavs were again on the defensive as the Germans resumed their advance. The fortified posts were restored, and the churches were reinstituted. Although Slavic risings continued throughout the century, the influx of settlers from as far away as Holland and Flanders and the construction of additional castles firmly established German control as far east as the Oder.

Without stretching the meaning of the term to the breaking point it is impossible to characterize the political and military structure of medieval Germany as "feudal." Only in the Rhineland, where French (or Frankish) influence was strong, did feudalism prevail. Elsewhere it spread very slowly and was so modified by pre-existing institutions or contemporary situations as to be scarcely recognizable. The tradition of infantry service that persisted among the Saxons, and the peculiarly German class of unfree "knights," the *ministeriales*, are instances of nonfeudal elements in German military organization. When, in the second half of the twelfth century, Frederick I (Frederick Barbarossa) attempted to establish a regular feudal hierarchy, feudalism was already breaking down in the England of Henry II and the France of Philip II Augustus, where the crown was assuming an ever increasing responsibility for military affairs. But although German military institutions were only partially feudalized, battlefield tactics were similar to those employed generally throughout western Europe. The principal reliance was on heavy-armed troopers, such as those who defeated the Hungarians on the Lech, but it was the failure of Frederick I, even though he had military talent, to appreciate the potential of good infantry that brought about the disaster at Legnano.

Conclusion

A survey which covers nearly five centuries and an area stretching from the Atlantic to the Orontes does not suggest meaningful generalities about the nature of military feudalism. Conclusions that would be applicable to one time and place probably would be completely inaccurate if applied to another place at another time, or even to the same place at another time. It would, for example, be equally difficult to make generalizations about the military developments in western capitalistic society since the beginning of the sixteenth century. Military history has, however, a continuity of its own, and the problems which confront those charged with the raising, maintaining, and employment of armed formations, are much the same except in emergencies, regardless of the social and economic systems that support them. Men have to be found who are willing to fight, and the rewards or recompense must be sufficiently attractive to make the risk of life and limb seem worthwhile, unless a government is sufficiently strong to compel men to perform military service. In the Middle Ages, few governments, except in comparatively small, closely knit communities, were able to resort to compulsion. And, until the end of the twelfth century, the states that could command popular support were not feudal. The Old English kingdom before its demise in 1066 and the communes of northern Italy after about 1150 were able to put their nonfeudal levies into the field with some confidence. It is noteworthy that William the Conqueror and his immediate successors did not hesitate to employ the Anglo-Saxon fyrd in foreign as well as domestic campaigns, and that the Holy Roman emperors came to grief in their attempts to impose imperial control by military force on the cities of the Lombard League.

What, then, can be concluded about the nature of what is loosely called feudal warfare? There seems to be no significant difference in the arms and armor used in France north of the Loire, in Crusader Syria, or in Christian states south of the Pyrenees. Castles appear to have been as abundant in the Midi, where most of the land was held allodially, as they were in Norman England, where all land, except that held in free alms, owed knight service. What was the difference between an unscrupulous tenant like Robert de Bellême, who forfeited his English lands for rebellion, and the equally unprincipled Cid, who could kiss his king's hands for favors received and then strike out on his own? The answer has to be: there was very little difference, except in strength of character and opportunity. Numerous questions can be formulated to indicate some of the work that must yet be done in the field of medieval military history.

It should be fairly obvious that the term "feudal" has customarily been applied far too loosely to the military procurement systems and operational procedures employed between the mid-seventh and late twelfth centuries. These must be examined in the light of conditions existing at the time, rather than according to the rigid definitions of legal and institutional historians. It should be kept in mind that during these centuries—but by no means only then—rulers and military commanders, who were frequently identical, conducted the affairs of state, raised armies, and led them on campaign and in battle according to no set legal, logistical, or tactical formulae. With the available means they tried whatever they thought might work.

Furthermore, as Bloch has noted, feudal armies were never recruited exclusively from the feudality, and it must also be obvious that military service was more widespread among the members of western society than is sometimes alleged. To think of medieval society as rigidly divided into "those who pray, those who fight, and those who work" is to have a totally misleading conception of the Middle Ages. There never was a time in this so-called feudal age when men of the lower classes were not to be found performing valuable—often invaluable—military services. All the infantry formations were drawn from these classes, as were the carpenters, the smiths, the carters, and all those whose services keep an army operational. Nor can it even be said that mounted service was ever the monopoly of a single class. In the Christian states of Spain, the nonnoble knights constituted one of the most important sources of military manpower, as they did in the communes of central and northern Italy. The mounted sergeants of England and France, while they do not seem to have been so numerous a class as the nonnoble knights of Spain and Italy, are frequently mentioned. Certainly they did not constitute part of the aristocracy. In Germany the peculiar development of the *ministeriales* put even the unfree serf on horseback for military service. And always there was the ubiquitous mercenary, of dubious origins, who was willing to sell his sword to the highest bidder. Limitations on the length and place of service of feudal troops encouraged rulers to seek other sources of recruitment; to the extent that their resources permitted, they hired professional soldiers whenever possible. The mercenary was likely to be better trained and better led, and as long as his pay was forthcoming, he was willing to fight anywhere, at any time.

It would be difficult, if not impossible, to cite a battle between armies composed entirely of feudal troops. Although major reliance was on the heavy-mailed horseman, the infantry was not despised. Specialists such as archers, crossbowmen, and engineers were always in demand, and Frankish commanders in Syria worked out a tactical system in which the infantry played an essential role.

The period of transition to mounted service in the eighth and early ninth centuries coincided with an economic crisis and a decrease in the amount of money in circulation. Kings and magnates were compelled to pay their soldiery with whatever wealth they had. There are indications that in some relatively prosperous areas military expenses continued to be met on a cash basis; other lords were able to maintain their armed bands as household troops or as castle garrisons. Still others made revocable land grants to individual warriors in return for military service.

At this stage there was no discernible difference between the mounted soldiers who received their wages in cash, those who were maintained as household troops, and those who received military benefices as compensation. All must be regarded as professionals who fought for a living. Their social status was amorphous, and even serfs could be assimilated into the military class. As late as the reign of Henry II of England, the two knights of Nicholas fitz Harding, who between them held three virgates of land, could hardly be regarded as influential people. (A virgate was twenty to thirty acres.) There seems to have been no limit to the amount of service that could be exacted from the military tenants, as the length of many campaigns testifies. During the occupation of England, active duty must have been almost continuous for many contingents. It was only when the land and military status became hereditary and the knight became a member of an aristocratic society that a difference developed between the knight and the often scorned mercenary. The knight as landholder acquired interests that were incompatible with those of the knight as soldier, and he sought to limit his military responsibilities as much as possible. He thus became a part-time soldier at best, and consequently a less efficient one. This explains in part why mercenaries were so widely employed.

Armies, between the eighth and the twelfth centuries, were extremely small by modern standards. Great enterprises were undertaken with forces that today appear ridiculously small. The army with which William of Normandy conquered England numbered perhaps as many as 7000 men, compared with the 52,000 commanded by the duke of Marlborough at Blenheim (13 August 1704). To defend his realm against converging English and imperial armies in 1214, Philip II of France put perhaps 27,000 men into the field, divided into two armies. At the end of the

United States Civil War (1861–1865), the southern Confederacy was crushed between Major General George C. Meade's Army of the Potomac (125,000) and Major General William T. Sherman's 60,000. Feudal armies, of course, cannot be compared with the mass armies of millions mobilized for the great wars of the twentieth century, but the army of 3700 men mustered by Prince Roger of Antioch for the disasterous campaign of 1119 might be compared with the more than 500,000 United States troops in South Vietnam in 1969. Sicily was overrun by armies that contained fewer than a thousand knights. The largest army ever mustered for the defense of the Latin kingdom of Jerusalem (1183) numbered no more than 15,000. Not until the beginning of the thirteenth century could it be said with any confidence that any western European monarch could put as many as 25,000 men into the field at one time.

Reliable evidence as to the size of particular armies is hard to come by. Several factors operated to keep their numbers minimal. The population of western Europe was much smaller than it had been in the days of the Roman Empire, and a far larger percentage of this population was engaged in the production of necessary foodstuffs than is the case today. There simply was not enough surplus manpower to staff large armies, nor was there surplus food with which to supply them. Much of Europe was covered by vast forests and stretches of wasteland; Spain and Syria were semiarid. Armies which made no provision for a commissariat had to live off the country through which they marched. If even so small an army as that of William the Conqueror had to march on two, or even three, roads in relatively prosperous England in order to procure sufficient food and forage (October–December 1066), can it be believed that 100,000 men could be supported on campaign in Andalusia, or 115,000 in the Po Valley? The figures supplied by the chroniclers are valueless, and only occasionally does a well-informed participant, such as Walter the Chancellor of Antioch, throw some light on the true state of military affairs.

Medieval generals are often faulted for lack of imagination and for their almost total reliance on the striking power of the heavy-mailed cavalry. The criticism is justified if relying on the best trained and most effective element then in existence can be called a fault. But to insist that the frontal cavalry charge was the sole tactical expedient of feudal generals is to ignore the evidence that can be found about literally scores of engagements. Medieval commanders did not have at their disposal permanent units that had drilled and fought together for long periods of time. Each army differed in composition and combat effectiveness from every other army, and a commander never knew until the muster was complete just what he would have to work with in order to achieve the objectives of a particular campaign. He had no permanent staff, and each army must have been organized on an *ad hoc* basis, often on the battlefield itself. Many of the troops were poorly trained and equipped. This was especially true of infantry levies, although those of Latin Syria, Christian Spain, and the Lombard cities were steady enough, and in other instances infantry contingents fought well. Under the circumstances it is not surprising that orders of battle and tactical movements tended to be simple. One has only to look at the opening engagements of the United States Civil War to see what can happen when complex maneuvers are attempted with untrained troops.

A common practice was to divide the available force into three divisions, with a tactical reserve provided on occasion. This practice was, however, by no means universal, and numerous variations were cited. Nor was there any standard method of combining the infantry and cavalry units. At Hastings, each of Duke William's three divisions contained both infantry and cavalry; the papal army at Civitate (1053) had one wing of infantry and a second of mounted troops; at Lincoln (1141) both armies were drawn up with the dismounted troops in the center and cavalry on each wing. The most common order of battle was that of three divisions in line, but engagements in which one or both contestants posted their divisions one behind another were not unknown; occasionally, in Frankish Syria, the divisions appear to have gone into action in echelon. At Tenchebrai (1106), King Henry I of England provided for a tactical reserve, as did King David I of Scotland at the Standard (1138), but more often, all troops were placed in the line of battle. Tenchebrai is remarkable also for King Henry's inclusion of a flanking detachment in his order of battle, but many other battles were decided when one wing of an army, having disposed of the enemy to its immediate front, intervened on the flank, as at Nocera (1132). Ambushes and feigned flights also figured in the repertoire of medieval generals as early as Henry the Fowler's repulse of the Hungarians at Riade (933). Among the Normans in particular, the knights never showed any reluctance to get off their horses and fight on foot as infantry, as they did at Tenchebrai, the

Standard, and Lincoln. European commanders, even feudal ones with what may be regarded as a feudal outlook, were able to adapt themselves and the forces at their disposal to as great a variety of conditions as their ancient and modern counterparts.

R. S. Hoyt observed that if "feudalism be understood to be essentially and above all a 'system' of tenures supporting military service, and if every other kind of arrangement by which rulers or lords obtained military service is understood to be 'non-feudal' or even 'anti-feudal' then it could be reasonably argued that medieval European society was never feudal—at least not completely or 'perfectly' feudal." [1] From the standpoint of the military historian it would be difficult to disagree with this conclusion. Feudal commanders were never entirely dependent on feudal military resources.

Throughout the Christian west during this period of nearly five centuries, response to military challenge was remarkably uniform. Arms and equipment varied little from one country to another. Battlefield tactics were much the same regardless of how the armies were recruited. What is not often noted is that with these troops and these tactics, European commanders were able to undertake successful offensive campaigns against nonfeudal states. After beating off the assaults of the Vikings and Hungarians, the armies of "feudal" Europe were able, between the end of the tenth century and the beginning of the thirteenth, to conquer England, southern Italy, and Sicily, to establish and maintain a bridgehead in the Middle East, to wrest large territories from the Moors in Spain, and to

[1] Robert S. Hoyt, "The Iron Age of English Feudalism," *Journal of British Studies,* II (1963), 27–28.

extend the frontiers of Latin Christendom eastward at the expense of the Slavs—no mean achievement. Medieval generals were surely as capable as commanders during any other period in history; and whatever their shortcomings in training and discipline, the troops, *milites peditesque,* were not lacking in fighting qualities.

Bibliographic Note

The reader who attempts to pursue further the military history of feudal Europe will soon discover that it is necessary to understand the nature of feudal society in more detail than is presented here. The literature on the subject is voluminous, but three studies must be regarded as indispensable: F. L. Ganshof's *Feudalism*, trans. Philip Grierson (2d Eng. ed.; New York, 1961); Marc Bloch's brilliant synthesis, *Feudal Society*, trans. F. L. Manyon (Chicago, 1961); and Sir Frank Stenton's *The First Century of English Feudalism, 1066–1166* (2d ed.; Oxford, 1961). The only general survey of medieval warfare in English is Sir Charles Oman's *A History of the Art of War in the Middle Ages* (2 vols.; London, 1924), which is still useful although some of his assumptions have since been disproven. Those who have a command of French or German would profit from reading Ferdinand Lot's *L'Arte Militaire au Moyen Age en Europe et dans le Proche Orient* (2 vols.; Paris, 1946) or the third volume of Hans Delbrück's magisterial *Geschichte des Kriegskunst im Rahmen der Politische Geschichte* (6 vols.; Berlin, 1920–1932). The general military institutions and accomplishments of the Normans in England and in Sicily and Syria between 1050 and 1100 are admirably summarized in chapters iii, iv, and ix of D. C. Douglas' *The Norman Achievement, 1050–1100* (Berkeley, Calif., 1969).

Specialized monographs tend to concentrate on periods later than the one treated here. A noteworthy exception is R. C. Smail's *Crusading Warfare (1097–1193)* (Cambridge, 1956), the very model of what such a study should be and probably the best work on any phase of medieval warfare that has been written. It would be impossible to list all the books and articles dealing with particular aspects of warfare in the feudal period; the following citations should, therefore, not be considered exhaustive, but only as suggestive of future study. Feudal warfare in England is covered in detail from both the institutional and operational points of view by C. W. Hollister in *The Military Organization of Norman England* (Oxford, 1965) and by John Beeler in *Warfare in England, 1066–1189* (Ithaca, N.Y., 1966); Norman operations in Ireland are detailed in the second chapter of G. A. Hayes-McCoy's *Irish Battles* (London, 1969). French military developments in the late twelfth century are treated minutely by Edouard Audouin in *Essai sur l'Armée Royale au Temps de Philippe Auguste* (Paris, 1913). Modern discussion of individual actions, however, must be dug out of works that are not primarily devoted to military matters, as were, for example, the conflicting reconstructions of the battle of Cassel cited in the text. Studies of monograph length are lacking for Italy, but some idea of the problems that need to be dealt with may be gained from K. F. Drew's "The Carolingian Military Frontier in Italy," *Traditio*, XX (1964), 437–447; and D. P. Waley's "Combined Operations in Sicily, A.D. 1060–

1078," *Papers of the British School of Rome,* XXII (1954), 118–125, and "The Army of the Florentine Republic from the Twelfth to the Fourteenth Century," in *Florentine Studies,* ed. Nicolai Rubenstein (London and Evanston, Ill., 1968) pp. 70–108. Waley's book-length works, *The Italian City Republics* (London, 1969) and *The Papal State in the Thirteenth Century* (London, 1961), also provide much useful data.

A great deal of information about the military aspects of society in southern France and Christian Spain can be gleaned from A. R. Lewis' *The Development of Southern French and Catalan Society, 718–1050* (Austin, Tex., 1965). The most recent survey in English of military institutions in the various Spanish kingdoms is that of Elena Lourie, whose "A Society Organized for War: Medieval Spain," *Past and Present,* No. 35 (Dec. 1966), 54–76, provides a good starting point. The latest scholarship on feudal and military institutions is summarized in the papers contained in *Les Structures Sociales de l'Aquitaine, du Languedoc et de l'Espagne au Premier Age Féodal* (Paris, 1969). About actual operations, however, there is little of a specific nature to be found. Oman's treatment of Spanish affairs begins only with the Navarette campaign (1367); while many helpful details can be found in such books as Ramón Menéndez Pidal's *The Cid and His Spain,* trans. Harold Sutherland (London, 1934), the fact remains that these were not written to provide military information.

Similarly, there is no readily available survey of the military history of the medieval kingdom of Germany. Although some of his concepts have since been modified, James Westfall Thompson's *Feudal Germany* (Chicago,

1928) still provides the most exciting and challenging view of the medieval German *Drang nach Osten.* In Peter Munz's *Frederick Barbarossa* (London, 1969) can be found the latest interpretation of that monarch's political and military policies.

The fairly recent discovery that the mercenary element in feudal armies was more important than historians had believed is reflected in such studies as Herbert Grundemann's "Rotten und Brabanzonen: Soldner-Heere im 12. Jahrhundert," *Deutsches-Archiv für Geschichte des Mittelalters,* V (1941–1942), 419–492; Jacques Boussard's "Les Mercenaires au XIIe Siècle: Henri II Plantagenet et les Origines de l'Armée de Métier," *Bibliothèque de l'Ecole des Chartes,* CVI (1945–1946), 1–36; and John Schlight's *Monarchs and Mercenaries* (Bridgeport, Conn., 1968). The closely related topic of the money fief is treated extensively in chapter v of Bryce D. Lyons' *From Fief to Indenture* (Cambridge, Mass., 1957).

Castles have always held an attraction which is amply illustrated by the extensive literature on the subject. A good introduction to the fascinating subject of military architecture is *A History of Fortification from 3000 B.C. to A.D. 1700* (New York, 1955), by Sidney Toy. This will enable the reader to understand the role of the feudal castle and its place in the development of fortifications. For a detailed discussion of the origins of the motte-and-bailey castle and its introduction into England, the authority is still Ella S. Armitage's *The Early Norman Castles of the British Isles* (London, 1912), although her interpretation has been challenged. (See Brian K. Davison, "The Origins of the Castle in England," *Archaeological Journal,* CXXIV (1967), 23–211). Books about English castles in

the Middle Ages are legion; one of the most authoritative
is R. Allen Brown's *English Medieval Castles* (London,
1954). The fortifications of Frankish Syria are treated at
length in Robin Fedden and John Thompson's *Crusader
Castles* (new ed.; London, 1957), and more recently in
Wolfgang Müller-Wiener's *Castles of the Crusaders*, trans.
J. Maxwell Brownjohn (New York, 1967). The early military architecture of Spain is rather superficially dealt with
by Alberto A. Weissmüller in *Castles from the Heart of
Spain* (New York, 1967). The motte-and-bailey structures
of the heartland of the old Frankish state receive exhaustive treatment in Michael Müller-Wille's *Mittelalterliches
Burghügel ("Motten") im Nördlichen Rheinland* (Cologne, 1966).

A brief but lively introduction to the siege warfare of
medieval times is provided by Philip Warner's *Sieges of
the Middle Ages* (London, 1968). While Warner is concerned primarily with English warfare, siege techniques
were much the same throughout the Christian west. An
interesting essay on the construction and use of military
engines is to be found, in addition to work on the crossbow, in Sir Ralph Payne-Gallwey's *The Crossbow* (reprint
of 1903 ed.; London, 1958). Armor and weapons are dealt
with by Claude Blair in *European Armour, circa 1066 to
circa 1700* (New York, 1959) and by R. Ewart Oakeshott
in *The Archaeology of Weapons: Arms and Armour from
Prehistory to the Age of Chivalry* (London, 1960). The
introduction of the stirrup, which made the feudal knight
possible, is traced in detail by Lynn White, Jr., in "Stirrup,
Mounted Shock Combat, Feudalism, and Chivalry," in
Medieval Technology and Social Change (Oxford, 1962).

The fact that most medieval chronicles were written in

Latin need not discourage the reader who may wish to learn something about the nature of the sources from which the history of the Middle Ages and its military institutions and practices must be reconstructed. Many of the chronicles are available in good English translations, and some have been published in inexpensive paper-back editions. (See Richard Kay and Elizabeth Atkinson's *The Middle Ages in Paper-Back* [Lawrence, Kans., 1969]). A small sampling will indicate the range of materials that should be obtainable in any good library. Einhard's classic *Life of Charlemagne* (Ann Arbor, Mich., 1960) is one of the principal sources for the military history of the Frankish empire; *History of Deeds Done beyond the Seas,* by Archbishop William of Tyre, ed. and trans. E. A. Babcock and A. C. Krey (New York, 1943), is the major authority for the history of Frankish Syria between the first and third crusades. The English civil wars of Stephen's reign are recorded in the anonymous *Deeds of Stephen,* ed. and trans. K. R. Potter (London, 1955). Bishop Otto of Freising supplies much detail about the early years of the reign of his illustrious nephew in *The Deeds of Frederick Barbarossa,* trans. C. Mierow (New York, 1966). This list could be extended to include most of the chronicles dealing with Saxon and Norman England, and many from such regions as the Elbe frontier, Crusader Syria, Christian Spain, and the Low Countries. The military history of feudal Europe, so long neglected by scholars, offers a challenge to the student, whatever his level of knowledge.

Index

WARFARE IN FEUDAL EUROPE
730-1200

Designed by R. E. Rosenbaum.
Composed by Vail-Ballou Press, Inc.,
in 11 point linotype Caledonia, 3 points leaded,
with display lines in Weiss Series III and Weiss Roman.
Printed letterpress from type by Vail-Ballou Press,
on Glatfelter Offset Vellum, 60 pound basis.
Bound by Vail-Ballou Press
in Interlaken AL1 book cloth
and stamped in All Purpose foils.